# Great Expectations of a Hopeless Romantic

# Great Expectations of a Hopeless Romantic

Elizabeth Cody Newenhuyse

VICTOR BOOKS
A DIVISION OF SCRIPTURE PRESS PUBLICATIONS INC.
USA CANADA ENGLAND

Edited by: Barbara Williams
Cover Design by: Scott Rattray
Cover Illustration by: Marilyn King

---

**Library of Congress Cataloging-in-Publication Data**

Newenhuyse, Elizabeth Cody.
Great expectations of a hopeless romantic / by Elizabeth Cody Newenhuyse.
p. cm.
ISBN 1-56476-096-0
1. Newenhuyse, Elizabeth Cody. 2. Married women–United States–Biography. 3. Marriage–Religious aspects–Christianity. I. Title.
HQ536.N52A3 1993
306.81–dc20 92-43009
CIP

---



1 2 3 4 5 6 7 8 9 10 Printing / Year 97 96 95 94 93

## DEDICATION

To Fritz—my first, last, and only husband

## ACKNOWLEDGMENTS

To Amanda, who ran in and out and provided healthy distraction while Mom was working;

To Curtis Lundgren and Bruce Zabel, my agents and friends who told me, "Go for it!"

To Barb Williams, Greg Clouse, and Linda Holland, patient and encouraging editors;

To "the group"—Diane, Charlene, and Jan—my lifeline to sanity some days;

And to Fritz, who made this and lots of other things possible,

My deepest gratitude.

CONTENTS

## FALL



## WINTER



## SPRING AGAIN

# INTRODUCTION

A few months ago a couple in our church renewed their vows on the occasion of their twenty-fifth wedding anniversary. They did it during the morning worship service, and it was moving to hear these two veterans repeat the words of the ancient ceremony with conviction, as though they knew *exactly* what was meant. When the pastor came to the "in plenty and in want" line, wife Sandy grinned up at husband Roger as if to say, "We've been there, haven't we, my love?"

I thought, *These people are heroes. Authentic heroes.* Forget the sports stars, the celebrity pastors, the politicians and TV personalities. When you can stay married twenty-five years, through seasons of warmth and seasons of chill, in an era that defines marriage as only one of many lifestyle alternatives—that's heroism.

My husband, Fritz, and I are a long way from the

quarter-century mark. God willing, we'll get there and far beyond. You couldn't quite call us "heroes" yet—we're still working out the bugs, as you'll see in some of these stories. But, after salvation, my marriage is the most precious gift God has sent. I hope you feel the same way about your marriage, and that's why I wrote this book: to encourage and strengthen you.

This is a book about us, but, I hope, it's also a book about *you.* Maybe you'll see yourself in some of the anecdotes. Maybe you'll discover that you're not the only one who struggles with money, or clutter, or a too-busy schedule. Above all, I hope you'll see how God is at work even in the smallest details of a marriage.

You may have been married a long time. Or maybe, like us, you're working toward it. If so, you're doing a very great and important thing, and God smiles at your efforts and is upholding you every step of the way, through every season.

My prayer is that this book will help you.

*Elizabeth Cody Newenhuyse*
*Wheaton, Illinois*

# *SPRING*

# *IN THE BEGINNING...*

I WAS SO CERTAIN whom I was going to marry. He had curly dark-auburn hair, fierce blue eyes under bushy eyebrows, a ruddy complexion. Bearded. Stocky but not too big. At barely five-four I didn't want to be loomed over. He would wear sweaters and sportcoats and caps and maybe be something Celtic. Witty, passionate, with a soul of unplumbed depths. A writer or poet, like me. We would live in a cottage in the country or by the sea. Somewhere.

Only I hadn't met him yet.

When the phone call came to invite me to a new church singles group that was being formed, I hemmed and hawed. "I'll see," I said. I didn't think I would know anybody. *Who of interest goes to church groups?* I thought. But my mother said, as mothers do (I know because I use that line now), "Why not give it a try?"

Well, I went, wearing what in those days passed for my dress-up outfit, meaning slacks that weren't jeans. The church basement fellowship room was crowded with people, of whom I knew exactly one. I didn't even know the minister, who had come while I was in college. We milled about for a while and I secreted myself behind or at least near a curtain and nodded politely when addressed.

When the minister heartily called us to sit down, it was time for introductions; and, in the way of such gatherings, we had to say something interesting about ourselves, maybe our favorite Beatle or something. I forget. But one of the guys said, "I'm Fritz Newenhuyse."

Fritz Newenhuyse? The All-Conference high school football and track star? He had been an outstanding senior when I was a lowly sophomore. In a school of near 5,000, he would not have remembered me. What was he doing here? I vaguely knew that his family went to our church. But it was a large church.

I looked up. He was blond, had a mustache, wore a nice green pullover and plaid pants. I supposed I could forgive him the plaid pants. This was, after all, the early seventies. He said he had been teaching and was temporarily living with his mother.

Near the end of the evening, I needed to use the facilities, but I did not know where they were. (I had been away from church for longer than I now care to admit.) Fritz was talking to someone, a girl. Naturally; he probably knew everybody there. But he looked approachable, like the popular guy who was nice to the outcasts. I asked him where the ladies room was, and he told me.

Afterward he asked me if I needed a ride home. I didn't; but I planned on needing one next time.

I was not really interested in him. I was going to marry a bearded Celt and move to England, remember. This was a mere way station. On the other hand, I didn't exactly have a lot of live options.

The next time he took me home. I liked his car, a yellow Toyota (which figures prominently in a subsequent narrative). It was late; my parents had gone to bed. Remembering a book I had read where the heroine cooked something and the man she was interested in viewed it as a declaration of romantic interest, I asked if he was hungry.

Fritz is always hungry. Then and now. He is also polite. "Sure," he said.

I fixed him a sandwich. Not just any sandwich, but my patented Sodium Nightmare creation: ham, cheese, mayo, pickle, mustard, lettuce, catsup, butter, sliced tomato on cracked-wheat bread. He sat in the breakfast area and ate. "Wow," he said. "This is really good."

I really liked the idea of entertaining a nice Christian guy. I was also lonely, and I learned, though he never admitted it, that he was. He started driving me home on a regular basis. We enjoyed talking to each other and would sit out in my driveway in the car for a long time, chatting, finding out how much we had in common, which was a lot. Then he would walk me to the front door. Once we looked at the stars. "That's Jupiter," I told him. "Aren't the stars beautiful?"

Some guys are sort of slow on the uptake. "Yes," he said seriously. "They're beautiful tonight."

Beat.

I waited. Slowly, I realized how much I was enjoying looking at his face, the slight network of smile lines around his eyes, the pleasing regularity of his blond features.

Nothing happened. I sighed and said, "Well, good night."

"Good night."

We started going out together from time to time, not just seeing each other at the singles group, which in any event was suffering the usual attrition such groups encounter and in time would dwindle to about six in attendance, about enough for a decent board game, and—after Fritz and I were solidly established as We—eventually peter out entirely. God's mysterious ways!

This is how the earth moves, with little tectonic shifts too small to be detected except on the sensitive scale of the heart. The smiles start adding up; the phone calls keep coming; and a person becomes necessary to your being. A real person, a kind guy who won't hurt you and has a lot to say. Not the bard of my dreams (although Fritz had, in his dreamy youth, written some creditable poetry), but a good and kind man who would do no harm, a man who had secret springs in his soul worth exploring.

It took him a little longer, as it often does with men. That's OK, I was romantic enough for us both. He'd come around and really notice Jupiter.

Let me tell you how it happened. Or let him tell it. He had been away visiting relatives . . .

"I pined for you the whole time I was in North Dakota," he would say later. "I thought about you all the time and couldn't wait to see you. So as soon as we got home I drove over to your house. You came to the door and you'd *changed*—new haircut, new clothes, you were losing weight—and I KNEW."

Who says beauty is as beauty does?

From then on, it was no longer a question of if, but when. We had a long road ahead of us. I had encouraged him in an old dream of going to seminary and entering the ministry, and we agreed we didn't want to start our marriage broke and living in school housing in a marginal neighborhood. "I'll wait for you," I told him when he started seminary.

Great expectations. Mighty dreams.

Nearly twenty years later, I think about those bright hopes, the springtide of a romance. I have heard it said that every now and then every couple ought to look back on their courtship, the Eden of their relationship when everything was so new. It is so easy for Eden to slip away. It is so easy to forget how it felt when the two of you exchanged a look and you realized that he was *seeing* you for the first time.

Here I sit now. Saturday. My husband is off helping a church family move. Our second-grader is playing with a friend. Our insurance man just called with details about a new policy we're considering. We all just got haircuts.

Details, details. But if you look hard at each one, they shine like little stars, with the brilliance of hopes fulfilled, dreams come to fruition, the scent of a spring that somehow lingers throughout the seasons of a marriage.

I guess I am a hopeless – or hopeful – romantic. I love storybook endings. When I'm watching a movie and the hero and heroine part, I fume: "Don't give him up!" I believe that love should culminate – not end – in marriage; and I guess I think that there really is that one person God has in store for each of us.

Soon, that person will be pulling in the driveway, exhausted from a strenuous day of lifting crates of books. He'll need a cold drink and a happy greeting.

Maybe I'll even fix him a sandwich.

# *WHEN THE OWL CAME*

WHAT *IS* IT ABOUT OWLS?

We saw one last night, about sunset. Amanda spotted it first. "Look," she said, pointing at an elm tree. "An owl or a hawk. I saw it flying. It went right above my head!"

A great dark shadow perched about halfway up, arching his head eerily. Maybe he thought we were prey. I could see his "ears" silhouetted against the western sky. A great horned owl! I had heard them in the North Woods of Wisconsin, and seen them pursued by crows in daylight, but had never come so close to one.

I looked at Fritz to make sure he was watching. He was. I'm not sure what we were waiting for, but the owl held us. I had heard that if you hoot at owls, they will call back, so I experimented with what I thought was a fairly accurate "Huh-who-who-who." The owl moved a bit but remained silent.

The sky was darkening quickly—a good thing, because we were sitting by my mother's driveway, in full view (and earshot) of all passersby. If anyone had noticed they would have thought we were waiting for E.T. to land, or maybe watching for the end of the world like one of those nineteenth-century sects.

The odd thing was, I had heard a screech owl at home late the night before. Here you think owls are practically extinct, a vanishing part of the world's wildness, then the wildness comes gliding back at you on silent wings. Two different owls in two different places. It felt portentous, somehow.

My neck was growing stiff and bugs were starting to bite. The owl hadn't moved. I wanted it to do something, perform, swoop down on a luckless meadow mouse, or hoot or something, but I knew owls could remain motionless for a long time. Owls aren't obliging, like chickadees who will talk back or butterflies who will land on you. The owl, governor of the night, does what he will, and it is never predictable. Once, years ago when I worked in downtown Chicago, I saw an owl outside the window. A dense fog swathed the high-rises by the lake, and suddenly out of the clouds a bird perched on the ledge outside the office window, sixteen stories up. I moved closer and saw that it was a small black-and-brown owl, possibly a youngster who had gotten disoriented in the fog. The bird stared at me with yellow eyes and then flew off. I cannot imagine where it had come from.

My mother went in to turn on the outside lights. The owl turned its head and watched her. Now I could see its markings. Definitely a great horned. Finally, reluctantly, I went in. " 'Night, owl," we said cleverly. *Thank you for existing. It is enough to know that you are.*

I love birds. I'm more fanatic about this than my husband. At various times in my life I have even kept a record, a "life list" of birds positively identified either by sight or by song. I had to teach Fritz to name the cardinal's whistle and hear the catbird mewing in the thicket. I know I embarrass him when we go for spring walks and I suddenly draw up short with a "wait!" So there we are, frozen in time and space, staring up into a blossoming magnolia tree where I have spotted a hard-to-identify warbler passing through. You never see a warbler head-on, but obliquely, peripherally. The best birds are always just out of reach, almost like the elusive, taunting embodiment of spring: Now you see me, now you don't! Catch me if you can!

Or I'll hear a mysterious fluting song and I'll go, "Listen! What IS that?" Listen! Listen! I have to *know!*

You either have this bird-urgency or you don't. My husband, like most people, doesn't; but I have taught him that birds are not just undifferentiated feathery things. They have names, habits, calls. Some stay around and some don't. The nighthawks flock and go in September; the slate-colored juncos return around October fifteenth; the male robin has a black head and the female does not.

Then there's the owl, in a league of his own.

What is it about owls? Even the name: *owl.* Short, Anglo-Saxon. I imagine them gliding over the downs of ancient Wessex.

I went outdoors later, looking for him again. Fritz had dozed off on the couch. Maybe I thought the great horned would still be sitting in the elm, waiting for his coterie of admirers to return so he could favor us with a hoot. It was almost moonrise. But he was gone; maybe the moon's rising was a signal that he had to be off and about his business.

"The owl left," I informed my sleepy mate.

"Oh," he said.

My husband, as I said, is only mildly fascinated by avian things. He prefers great heroic creations like the grizzly or the moose. Something a man can get hold of. But he will *try* to respond to my quizzing: "OK, what song was that?" He loves that part of me that is sort of whimsical and questing and flittery—birdlike.

For my part, I am only mildly interested in one of his passions—music. If it were up to him, our life at home would be accompanied by a perpetual soundtrack of tapes, an eclectic concert ranging from Frank Sinatra to Motown to the Bill Gaither Trio to the Voices of the Red Army. I get tired of constant sound. I don't have a tin ear and actually sing rather well, but music is not central to my life and being the way it is to Fritz's. When I'm home by myself it seems self-indulgent to play music, as if I were making myself a banana split at eleven in the morning and eating it while watching "Andy Griffith" reruns. I'm more likely to turn on radio news.

But when my husband is home, we play music. It's just the way it is. I bow to his interest the way he indulges mine, because his tapes represent something very special and particular about him. He'll say, "OK, what's playing now?" "Handel?" I say hopefully. "No, Bach." We learn from each other.

I haven't quite figured out this difference, his music, my music. It may be simple acceptance: You love it, it doesn't hurt anything or cost much money, so I will try to share it with you or at least let you love it without stepping on that love.

This is a very big and important thing to know about marriage, I suspect. Maybe even *the* biggest, over time. Let the other have his music. And please, try to love it a little . . . for the other's sake.

It's raining as I write this, and I'm not sure the owl will return tonight. If he does, I don't mind going outside by myself to stand vigil: On the Owl Patrol. I know people who walk around woods on freezing nights hooting, such is the magic of owls. Yes, Fritz will probably be inside, playing his music. But if the owl does come and call for us, I'll be sure to run and tell him. He's the first I would want to know.

# *WEST SIDE BREAKDOWN*

IT WAS EVERY SUBURBANITE'S nightmare.

We were driving on the expressway that bisects Chicago's West Side, a section of the city that most people would most assuredly not want to get lost in. Blocks and blocks of the area burned following the assassination of Martin Luther King, Jr., in 1968 and much of it is simply empty—vacant lots, abandoned houses, deserted streets. Every cliché in the world comes to mind when you think about the West Side, and most people try not to think about it very often, which is part of the West Side's problem. So there it sits with its unemployment and drugs and despair and danger, a place ignored and fled from.

The Eisenhower Expressway is as close as many

people get to the west side. They tore down some of the old neighborhoods to build it, at about the same time blacks were moving in there. Commuters stuck in rush-hour traffic stare straight ahead, or talk on their cellular phones, or talk back to the radio. Mostly their windows are rolled up and their doors are locked.

But on this April night it had started raining hard. Fritz and I were returning home from an evening with an old college friend. Back then we had a Toyota which had been built when "made in Japan" was synonymous with gimcracky souvenirs. The thing had a disconcerting way of wheezing to a halt at the most inopportune times. In intersections. On off-ramps. In zero weather. Once the shock absorbers fell off onto the street, and we had to go lurching into the nearest service station. The car, I am convinced, hated us and wished to place us in harm's way.

The rain poured, and the car, true to its vicious nature, started bucking and halting, and finally sputtered to a complete stop. Fritz was able to steer it onto the shoulder, where we sat. "What do we do now?" I asked. I knew he hadn't a clue as to what was wrong, but, as men do, he got out and peered under the hood and shook his head.

On such a night, no one was going to help us; and it was probably just as well, given the locale. "I'll have to go for help," said my brave knight.

I kissed him. "Be careful."

Off he ventured into the unknown terrors of a West Side Friday night. At least the rain would hold some of the terrors at bay, I thought as I watched him scale the embankment up to the overpass. He waved, and I looked hard at him, thinking, *I may never see him again.*

There is nothing that makes you feel more vulnerable than sitting on a freeway shoulder as cars speed by in a blur of headlights and a swish of tires on wet pavement. I sat, and thought, and sat, and thought, for an agonizingly long time. To compound the agony, I had drunk a fair amount of Coke and nature was calling rather insistently. I imagined my beloved being set upon by roving bands of thieves and brigands patrolling the mean streets. At best, I doubted whether he could find a service station or even a pay phone. Not for the first or last time, I thanked God that I was a person of the female persuasion: equality aside, when there is danger in the night, it is not the woman who risks herself. Not if there is a man who cares for her in the vicinity.

Finally, finally, the most welcome sight in the world, the flashing yellow lights of a tow truck, pulled up behind the faithless Toyota. My hero knocked on the window: "Get in the truck!" He introduced me to Mr. Raybon, a black man in rain gear. I climbed in the cab of the tow truck, and eventually we were on our way to Raybon's Standard.

As we drove, I looked for roving bands but saw nothing. The West Side seemed to be locked up tight. Raybon's was a brightly lit oasis in the midst of darkness. I made a dash to necessity, then returned to the service bay where another black man offered me a chair and some coffee. Queen Elizabeth could not have felt more royally treated. Johnny Carson was joking with Ed on black-and-white TV and while the men worked on the car, I half-watched Johnny and thought about a lot of things—how relieved I was, whether we would have to spend the week here while Mr. Raybon ordered parts from Yokohama or someplace (this was before Toyotas were made in U.S.A. with American labor and Japanese money), and how amazing all this was.

It turned out that somehow the rain had gotten on the distributor cap—apparently the engine was wide open to the elements—and the Raybon men put a sheet of cardboard over the grille and assured us that the simple repair should get us home safely, but we'd better get that distributor looked at pronto.

We did make it home. Fritz wrote Amoco customer relations, commending the service shown us by Raybon's, and received a nice letter back, informing him that Raybon's had been sent a special citation. I pictured it framed and proudly hung on the wall by the cash register. A few months later we traded in the Toyota for a great big gas-guzzling Pontiac that never broke down, even during the winter Chicago got something like a hundred inches of snow.

Some years (and about five cars) have passed since that April. I'm not sure Raybon's is still there—and I'm not sure, if the same thing happened to us today, that I would be telling you the same story. Life for the people of the West Side, and those who blunder onto its streets, has gotten a lot meaner and more dangerous than it was the night we were marooned on the Ike. And, safely ensconced twenty-five miles due west, we have become more cautious. More careful. Less adventurous.

But we still talk about "the time we broke down on the West Side."

*The time we . . .* Of that little phrase is the fabric of a marriage spun, and the things you remember aren't necessarily the stuff of Hallmark commercials. Remember the time we ate dinner at a downtown hotel and saw Muhammad Ali and you went up to him and asked him about Howard Cosell and he said, "Sometimes I wish I was a dog and Howard was a tree"? Remember our "honeymoon," when we both got stomach flu and had to stay home in bed and feed each other Jell-O and tea? Remember the extraordinarily large green bug in our bedroom in Elgin? Remember when we sat with your mother at your grandmother's wake? Remember the time last year when the tornado sirens went off and we took to the basement with candles and flashlights? We even carried the parakeets down in their cage, but we couldn't coax the dog down the stairs so you had to keep going upstairs to check on him? That afternoon we really thought that this was the Big One.

But they're *our* "times when." Specific, particular, known only by us. They're almost like secrets hidden in two hearts, secrets that we sometimes bring out and lovingly inspect and talk about and then return to their hidden places. Everyone has wedding stories; everyone speaks glowingly (and at length) of their childbirth experiences; everyone can talk about their first date or their first home or what they do on Christmas. Everyone goes for walks in the rain, looks at stars, snuggles in front of a fireplace. How many people can talk about the time one spouse was coming home on the train and got absorbed in a magazine article and didn't hear her stop called? The idiot, she had to jump off the train after it had started moving again and she took a flying leap onto the brick platform . . .

Ahem. Well. These memories matter, and sometimes it's the dangerous or dirty or humiliating memories that linger the longest, and you don't talk about them with anyone else because other people wouldn't get the joke or catch the significance. And, life being the way it is, we'll have more of these adventures to store up against those times of chill that come to all marriages. If nothing else, we'll have more to talk about.

Now, didn't I hear a funny noise in our latest car? Nah. Couldn't be. It was made in Japan.

# *THE MOM AND THE BOYFRIEND*

ALL RIGHT, CALL ME OLD-FASHIONED. But the other day when my daughter told me that "Nicole's mom has a new boyfriend, and Nicole has to stay at her grandma's because her mom is going out with the boyfriend," I was at once startled and sad. I wanted to close her ears and put my hands over her eyes and take away all the bad modern things that a child of her age picks up. "Great," Fritz, overhearing, muttered to himself.

Moms don't have boyfriends. Moms are supposed to have husbands, unless the husband is in heaven, like Grandpa Jake who died when Daddy was sixteen. Then it's OK not to have a husband, but you still remember him and keep his picture in your living room. That's what I would like to teach my eight-year-old. There's another boy in her class who never knew his father. Amanda thinks Ryan's daddy died when he was a baby, and I am content to let her think that.

We moved here when Amanda was an infant, crawling and hanging onto furniture and experimenting with language. In fact, she said her first "word," "uh-ee," the day we moved. A major reason behind the move was the urge to seek shelter for our child, to find a safe harbor where families are still intact and God is still taken seriously and you needn't fear the stranger on the street.

This town is all these things. It's friendly, reassuring, green. There's even a mini-rush hour on Sunday noons when all the churches empty out. On these spring days everyone walks and bicycles and says hello. And most children in our neighborhood live with both parents, who are usually in their first and, Lord willing, only marriage.

What's wrong with saying that's the way it should be?

But you can't build a protective bubble around an entire town. Once I read a science-fiction story where astronauts were exploring Venus and found it to be a world of eternal, continuous rain; so much rain that the color in the vegetation had washed out and everything was a drippy grey. They were beginning to go mad from the ceaseless pounding of the drops when they discovered giant domes in which someone had captured sunshine—warm, dry mini-worlds where a voyager could find hot towels, a change of clothes, comfortable chairs, multicourse dinners, even a blue sky. Sun Domes.

I want Amanda to live in a Sun Dome, at least for a few years. But on Earth, if not on Venus, bubbles have a way of cracking to let in the rain and muck from outside. Even in our town, there are little Nicoles whose mothers take up boyfriend after boyfriend—Nicole calls them her "daddies"—while the child is shipped out to grandma's so Mom can have a good time.

Maybe that sounds harsh, judgmental. Maybe I need to be more tolerant. Maybe I should get in step with the times. If everyone's doing it, doesn't that indicate some sort of societal shift? You can't turn back the clock.

The conversation continued.

Amanda and Nicole had been talking on the playground at school. Nicole had told my daughter about "sex." Sex. "Um, what did she say?" I asked, trying to remain offhand.

"It's when you love each other and hug and kiss," she said.

"Like I kiss Daddy. When you're married it's fun to do that sometimes," I said. "And—"

"Can I go play?"

"OK." Whew. That was close. Next time, though, I'm afraid she's going to get it right.

Like millions of other Christian parents, my husband and I talk about this a lot: How do we make sure our child embraces *our* values and not those of the world outside the dome? At the same time, how do we prepare her for real life? Should we tell her about sex now, or wait until it comes up? What about the influence of children like Nicole, growing up in a broken home? I've met Nicole's mother and like her. I don't want to say to my child, "You can only play with children whose parents are white-collar evangelical Protestant Christians, are in their first marriage, and go to church three times a week." I want my daughter to understand that we do live in a diverse society, and I want her to have compassion for those who are struggling, as I suspect Nicole's mom struggles. And who knows? Maybe the mom and the boyfriend will get married.

Still . . . I don't want my child to take divorce and moms-with-boyfriends for granted, as if these things were an everyday fact of life like right turn on red and recycling pop bottles. I want her to feel that divorce is WRONG, a terrible tragedy. When I was her age I knew only one kid whose parents were divorced. I wish things were like that today, but they aren't. So it falls on us, her parents, to teach her the way it's supposed to be in the sight of God.

"The Bible shouldn't be taken as a handbook for sexual behavior," say some voices in the church. Right. So what do we substitute? Our own good judgment?

As for me and my house, we will teach the Word. But equally important, my husband and I will try to live it – to embody to our child that it is the better way for a man and woman to live together in relative harmony and contentment for a lifetime. More than that, it's also doable.

It's real easy to slip on the "harmony" question. Even now, tears come to my eyes as I recall James Dobson's story of the wife and husband who were quarreling in the front seat of their car, exchanging hurtful words, while in the back seat their young son, forgotten, wept in fear. To argue in front of your child is a form of abuse and abandonment. She doesn't know that "Mommy and Daddy don't really mean it." All she knows is that the two people who form the mountains to her protecting valley seem not to like each other anymore. The mountains are crumbling.

I have, on occasion, said a discouraging word to my husband – in front of my daughter – and, always, have kicked myself afterward. Fritz and I try our best to keep our arguments "for adults only." When we kiss each other in front of Amanda, she may say "Eewww, mush," but her eyes shine. We're careful to build one another up to her – "Isn't Mommy pretty?" – or "Let's have the house all clean for when Daddy gets home!" In a prelude to more serious and graphic discussion, I tell her that hugging and kissing mean two people are IN LOVE, and when you're IN LOVE you get married.

Saccharin? Maybe. Maybe too a dose of saccharin is what this sour world needs.

Amanda is just poised on the edge of *knowing.* It won't be possible to seal her eyes and ears shut much longer. There'll be other Nicoles, other moms with boyfriends who come and go. Our prayer, Fritz's and mine, is that by then Amanda will have a clear vision for what is right, what is intended—and that in that vision, she'll see a couple of people who know what *real* romance is.

# *ME AND MY NOBLE ROMAN*

I SIT IN THE CORNER of the church sanctuary, in the shadow of a cross. I am barefoot and wrapped in a heavy robe. A group of children and their parents crowds around me expectantly.

"My name is Mary," I begin.

Good Friday. Our church is performing a children's play I have written and helped direct, loosely based on the stations of the cross. My husband stands at the front, wearing a Roman helmet, breastplate, sandals. I have cast him in the role of "Quintilius," a hard-bitten centurion who supervised the Crucifixion. He has played his part well, striding out with an arrogant expression, recounting how as a Roman he didn't care about the tangled religious controversies of "these people." He was just there to do his job, carry out his orders.

The children are spellbound. I recall the prophecy of a sword piercing my heart, Jesus commanding, "Woman, behold your Son!" It begins as a bit of amateur acting, a woman in a homemade bathrobe. But as my eyes search the audience's faces, as I continue speaking, I find myself choking up. My voice rises and becomes powerful as I say, "To the crowd, He was the Galilean, or the Messiah, or the threat to the peace. But He was also my Son."

I am so glad my husband is here to *be in* Holy Week with me. He stands soldierlike at his station, looking most Roman with his close-cropped hair and clean-shaven face. We're in this one together.

The week before I spoke at a women's breakfast on the meaning of Holy Week, on living the Passion of the Lord and not jumping ahead to Easter's glory. We are trying to do that this year. Church services. Family talks about the meaning of Jesus' death and resurrection. This weekend we are going to listen to the entire *Messiah.* Amanda has been watching the *Jesus* video over and over, in the way of children. We plan to eschew shopping and other such pursuits. Even Saturday house-cleaning will be done in the spirit of preparation for Sunday, the way Jewish housewives prepare for Passover.

And so we spent the long weekend quietly, thinking about these things. It rained all day Easter Sunday, a cruel blow since the holiday came late that year, at a time when one could reasonably expect fine weather. No matter; Amanda hunted eggs anyway (she knows who hid them but still enjoys the tradition, as do we). We spent the entire morning at church, lingering over the Easter buffet. I cooked an elaborate ham dinner for just us three.

We need these dramatic, tangible reminders of what God has done for us. It's so easy to take salvation for granted. It's so easy to take a believing spouse for granted—until I see the struggles some "unequally yoked" couples go through. And it's all too easy to get caught up in the mundane and blind ourselves to the holy, the transcendent.

Yes, in the end each of us stands alone before God. Yet to share a faith, and to help nurture that faith in the other, is an awesome responsibility. To serve together can be a joy. Like many women, I'm the "of course" person in our family. Nursery duty? Of course. Communion setup? We'll be there. Greet? Make coffee? Work on a committee? Point us in the right direction. (As you see, most of these activities are performed in the plural.)

Thus I had written the part of the centurion with my husband in mind, and he cheerfully went and rented a costume and practiced his lines: "Just another execution? I guess not. Because I looked up . . . and the Galilean was looking down at me, and there was something in His eyes. . . ."

And the wonder of it all is that thirty or so years ago, a crewcutted boy sat in a convention hall in downtown Chicago and heard Billy Graham challenge his listeners to see and believe, and that this boy made the long walk forward, all by himself, to claim the prize Jesus offers.

And the further wonder is that a young woman living just a few miles away from the youth would yield her life to the Lord, and that these two, we two, would be led to each other. It's as if the Lord said to each of us, "Here is a soul, bright and shiny. I place it in your hands for safekeeping until I decide it's time for the soul to come home."

That's the stiffest, and most humbling, charge I ever heard of. It means you think hard about how you treat the other person. It means you pray for and with them. It means you help them not to stumble. The other day we were at the supermarket, putting groceries in the car. Fritz said, "Did the checkout girl charge us for this milk in the bottom of the cart?" "I'm not sure," I said. "Better go back and tell her." As it turned out, he looked at the register tape and she had rung it up. But it's little things like that – helping the other be honest, be kind, be diligent in spiritual practices – that are involved in the care of a soul. In the same way Fritz will sometimes ask me, "Have you prayed today?" Sometimes I have, sometimes I haven't, but I always appreciate the gentle reminder.

Every now and then, it is salutary to step back from the daily grind and, in a sense, retreat together. Usually neither he nor I has that luxury. I'm always working. He's always working. Which is one reason I signed him up for centurion duty, because I knew that if I did not, he would spend

Good Friday catching up on chores.

After the service we changed back into street clothes. People crowded around saying how wonderful the program was and how we should try to market it to other churches. I felt a winged elation, not because I had written something so wonderful, but that the Holy Spirit had used it to touch people—and that my husband and I had shared in that touching.

# *GOOD-BYE, MRS. MURPHY*

I CAN'T BELIEVE IT. They tore down my school. *My* school, where I spent eight years. My school, where I learned my multiplication tables and got teased by Bob Kuenzel and won the sixth-grade spelling championship and fainted in the nurse's office. We drove by there a month or so ago, and all that was left was a pile of bricks. I could hardly bear to look.

The school was built in 1926, at least the original old part with the green walls and funny staircases and black-and-yellow tiled room where we would watch Encyclopedia Britannica movies with wavery soundtracks, or Forties-era physical education films featuring chubby girls in bloomers. I still remember the sound of the old projector rattling as the film ran off the reel at the end. The school's floors were pitted with the imprints of thousands of feet. In some classrooms they still used the ancient desks with inkwells. Many of the teachers seemed at least as old as the desks. The playground in those pre-liability insurance days was dangerous, concrete with high metal swings and slides and – horrors! – seesaws.

I guess they had a bad asbestos problem and the school had to go. They're building a modern new facility, low-slung, asbestos-free. It'll have computer labs and indoor carpeting and modern desks in friendly groupings instead of forbidding rows.

But will it feel the same? On rainy days the yellowish incandescent light fixtures lit the classrooms softly and made you feel cozy and safe inside. Fluorescent tubes don't do that. The clocks lurched forward with clicking sounds. One of the bus drivers was a farmer who had made a mint selling off most of his land for development. I remember the time his barn burned down, when I was in sixth grade. Everyone thought Marty Marks, the worst kid in school, had torched it. We KNEW he was going to go to reform school. Our suspicions were confirmed when he didn't come back in eighth grade. Now that I think about it, it could be his parents sent him to Catholic school.

Authority meant something in those days. We were appropriately scared of the principal, a tall, forbidding woman with salt-and-pepper hair and a deep voice. We *knew* she kept a spanking machine in a room whose door we never saw opened. Mrs. Murphy, unlike today's educators, didn't concern herself much with promoting self-esteem in her 800 charges.

I hate it that I can't go back there ever again.

I wanted to show my daughter Mom's school—not some heap of rubble. I wanted to show Fritz the school, walk the halls again, drop in on the school secretary, and bore her with stories of how I graduated from there thirty years ago and could I go look at my old classrooms?

Most people I know have similar vivid memories of their grammar-school days. High school is something many of us were glad to escape. We keep in touch with our college, or our college keeps in touch with us (even a fugitive from justice who has changed his name and undergone plastic surgery cannot escape his alumni fundraising mail). But there's a mystique about grade school, because while we're there we're literally getting *formed,* and the place that forms you stays with you. If you stay in one place, as I did, you keep many of the same friends – or enemies, or victims – year after year. And, of course, we older folk have excellent memories for things that happened in a previous geologic epoch.

Fritz is the same way. He can go on for hours about Hubbard Woods School and how his record for most chin-ups still stands and how he and Margy Everitt traded dogtags in fifth grade. (*Fifth grade? In 1957?*) The difference is, *his* school is still standing, and I'm having dreams about Avoca.

On the other hand, there's no camera better than the mental camera, and the image is brightened when you have someone to share it with. Both Fritz and I have strong powers of recollection, and we love trading those recollections. It was an early bond between us, growing up in the same place and swapping reminiscences like two old guys around a wood-burning stove in the general store. Pure memory has a power that photos, videos, home movies, scrapbook clippings cannot match.

The other day I was reading a column by Bob Greene in the *Chicago Tribune.* The man who developed the technology for instant replay on televised sports had died, and Greene was reflecting on how instant replay and other technologies have changed our perception of events. An event isn't "real," Greene said, until we've seen it recorded. We've lost our appreciation of the immediacy of something.

I tend to agree. I've already told you about some of Fritz's and my most memorable adventures—breaking down in the inner city, my jumping off the train. Needless to say, these adventures weren't filmed! (Thank heaven.) They exist in our shared memory and conversation.

Let them, and other stories, rest there. We've all heard stories of someone who goes back to visit her childhood home and finds it disturbingly small, changed, disappointing. The trees aren't as big as she remembered and there's a junk car sitting in the front yard. The present owners have redone the sunny kitchen of her childhood in garish orange-and-green wallpaper. She goes away sorry she ever stopped by.

Perhaps it would be that way had I returned to my grammar school. Maybe the school secretary would be brusque and annoyed at my intrusion. Maybe the yellow-and-black tiled room would have been redone into a computer lab long ago; maybe the old hanging fixtures would have been replaced by energy-efficient fluorescents. I'm *sure* they'd have put up new playground equipment.

Guess it's time to move on. Close the books on one season, look toward another. With Fritz. The past is a nice place to visit, but we really don't want to live there. There are too many exciting things going on in the present—*our* present.

"Our" school is now Hawthorne Elementary, just a few blocks away. It's considered to be the best in our town, a true neighborhood school; I can walk Amanda there. Lots of Christian teachers. They *do* promote self-esteem, but maybe that isn't so terrible, given the state of a lot of families today. Besides, the principal is still the Ultimate Disciplinarian, and I still see boys sitting in the office looking hangdog. Some things never change.

# *SUMMER*

# *CONSIDER THE PEONIES*

THIS IS ONE OF THOSE DAYS you would like to bottle and keep on the canning shelf in your basement, to uncork some February day when you need to smell some clover, hear the buzzing of bees, taste wild strawberries, feel the breeze ruffling your hair and a warm rushing creek between your toes. Is *anything* like June when June is acting like it's supposed to?

Around here, we get hot spells in June. I've never been to a graduation that didn't feel like I, and the lads and lasses in their suits and dresses, were turning slowly on a rotisserie. Sometimes it gushes rain in June. Or there's a drought. In June 1988 our lawn was already brown.

But today is perfect. The sun is way, way overhead. Light everywhere, all over the northern half of the world right now. The yellowjackets haven't come out to spoil the party. Enough warmth to penetrate my fast aging bones; enough breeze to keep away the sweat.

All I want to do is lie here on my chaise and sniff the air and sleepily think in little fragments. Our neighbor across the street has a big stand of peonies; the smell is drifting all the way over here. "Pinies" are such forward, flaunting flowers, big and so fragrant it's almost tacky. And, unlike roses, peonies are cheerful and forgiving, not thorny and demanding. You can ignore them and they still grow.

My husband picked me some ignored peonies from a back corner of our yard. I laugh to myself as I recall how he put them on the table in a vase and ants came crawling out all over the tablecloth. Can't have peonies without ants, I told him. He grinned and swatted the ants.

My husband, I think, is nice like a peony, not temperamental like a rose.

June, time of brides. I guess it's still the most popular wedding month. Imagine getting married on a day like this.

But *staying* married—it's like the difference between a hothouse floral arrangement and dependable perennials that come up year after year. Again, take the peony. All you have to do is divide it every few years, keep it watered, feed it, cut it back in fall. You wouldn't even have to do that much. It would still bloom for you, through frost and sleet and drought and the bad springs we get here. Roses have to be sprayed, trimmed just so, checked for aphids, given a special gourmet diet, even placed under cones when it gets cold. Like they have to have their own house. We have some roses we inherited when we moved in here and I ignored them, and now they're just a bunch of thorny stalks with a few listless blooms. They don't even smell good. It's their fault for being so hard to live with. If they're not careful, I'm going to dig them out and replace them with sod and throw them in a pile with dandelions. Serves them right. People who grow roses must have too much time on their hands, or they live someplace like Oregon.

I really like being married to my husband. He's easy to live with, not especially moody, and I can talk to him about anything, including my rambling theories about marriage and flowers.

He wears well. Peonies wear well; crabapple trees are even more durable. We have a big crab in our front yard. It's got to be twenty, twenty-five years old. It *towers* over the house now, spreading everywhere. A couple of summers ago we thought it was dying, that maybe some kind of worm or borer was devouring it from within. The leaves were scanty and fell off early. We talked about having it sprayed in the early spring.

Surprise! The next year it came in lusher than ever, full of deep-pink blooms. The leaves made a canopy an elm would be proud of. In the fall, the crabapples were so abundant you couldn't walk in the front yard without stepping on them so that there was a mashed carpet of fruit all over the grass. I was forever sweeping them off the side-walk. "Can you make crabapple compote?" Fritz asked. "You know, like cranberry sauce?" Some-times nature is extravagantly wasteful.

Crabs, I've been told, are bred to thrive in our hard winters and hot summers. We don't have the South's palm or orange trees. They won't grow here; the climate is too challenging and the soil wrong. We planted a spindly peach tree once, and all summer we had this little stick growing out of a patch of dirt. It was really sad, and finally we pulled out the stick and threw it away. Crabs, however, will grow and endure. One spring we had a near-tornado which tore down lots of branches from lesser trees—but our crab tree stood proud and untouched.

My husband is strong like our crab tree.

This isn't to say we have a no-maintenance marriage. Oh, no. We fuss over it, the way we fuss over our lawn.

And our lawn responds accordingly. Take care of your grass, and it will take care of you.

Like our marriage. I fuss over my husband, and he takes care of me. He brings me coffee in bed in the morning. I get up with him if he has to be somewhere early. He screens phone calls, saving me from dealing with telemarketers (and saving us money, as I have been known to fall for their entreaties: "I am handicapped. Will you buy my greeting cards?"). I let him have his childhood junk on his dresser—an old penny bank, a stein from Germany, a trophy. He'll buy me nylons if he's going to the store. I scrub the bathroom tile so he doesn't have to do it.

It's an ongoing pampering and cultivation. As with lawn care, it sometimes feels like *effort:* remember to compliment him on his tie. Be sure to get the kind of bath soap she likes. It doesn't always come naturally—but it sure pays off. And, unlike a lawn, a marriage doesn't go dormant during the winter.

But some periods are more green than others. When the dry times come, when the gray days set in, it's nice to have some of that care bottled up as a reminder of the sunshine and the flowers.

# *LAKE MINNETONKA DAYS*

TODAY WAS LIKE A SUMMER RESORT. I'm not sure why. We'd had a lot of rain, and my memories of childhood vacation spots have a lot to do with dampness—wet bathing suits on a line, looking for purple and red mushrooms in the woods, whiling away rainy days with Ping-Pong and card games. The air smelled like wet pine needles and motorboat fuel, and I thought about Lake Minnetonka days.

Lake Minnetonka is a big lake not far from the Twin Cities. Suburban sprawl has now overtaken the area, but time was when it was a resort destination, on the streetcar line from Minneapolis. Around the turn of the century, my Minnesota in-laws, the Holmquists, built several summer cottages in the hamlet of Greenwood City on the banks of St. Alban's Bay, frame houses with screened porches and (then) no indoor plumbing. Now they're surrounded by modern ranches and split-levels, and they look like gallant, aging holdouts against the new, like some upper-class women I know who have worn their hair in the same pageboy for forty years.

It was to St. Alban's Bay that my then-boyfriend brought me to ask me to be his bride. With relatives proximal, we stayed in separate bedrooms in Uncle Tiny's cottage. (He was called Tiny because his real name was Clarence. The only other Clarence I ever knew was nicknamed "Babe.") Tiny's place was yellow and teemed with mice; you could hear them tap-dancing in the attic at night. All the little feet sounded like mouse Rockettes. But at least Tiny's place had hot water; Uncle Harold's cottage, which we also visited once, did not and you had to boil water on an old black stove to wash up. Great-Grandma Holmquist, I was told, always reminded her many progeny, in her Swedish lilt, "Yer at the lake now! You mustn't be so par-tic-u-lar!" And my future mother-in-law told me cheerfully that it was all part of the vacation-land ambiance.

So too was the time we rowed to church. When Fritz tried to start his old station wagon, smoke spewed alarmingly from under the hood. We wanted to go to church, so with the "why not?" spirit of the young, we decided to take a boat across the bay to the village. However, there were no motorized craft to be had. So we took an old dinghy (I guess it was a dinghy, or maybe it was a skiff; anyway, it was wooden and had no motor) and Fritz rowed us to the Excelsior Community Church, where we were pleased to hear a fine sermon and, as visitors, were properly buttonholed by a couple of deacons and steered toward doughnuts.

We had an excellent time in the Twin Cities, where for some reason there are lots of redheads, and where you can see things like skywalks and the test kitchens where they make Bisquick and Hamburger Helper. (This was long before they opened the world's largest indoor mall in suburban Bloomington.) During all this revelry my now-husband could barely contain himself, dropping broad hints about a package he had tucked in his personal belongings and carried all the way from Chicago.

Just a couple of nights before we were due to leave, he said, "Want to go for a boat ride? It's a nice night." I was sitting around reading a women's magazine and said sure. He disappeared into his room for a moment, came back and said, "Ready!"

The month was June, a little too early for the onslaught of what has been called Minnesota's state bird—the mosquito. It was just dark outside. We got in the dinghy and he rowed out some yards from shore, where we sat, bobbing gently.

I don't remember all his exact words now. He talked about how we had been together for a long time, and how he couldn't imagine life apart from me. As at all moments I've had when emotions run deep and real and important, I was silent, almost tongue-tied. Then he drew out a small jeweler's box and, grinning, asked, "Will you marry me?"

Would I!

I nearly jumped across the boat. By the lights

from the houses on shore, he put the engagement ring on my finger – a diamond in a gold filigree setting we had agreed upon on a trip to Erickson Jewelers, run by a Korean probably named Kim, a few months previous. (Discounts for seminary students.)

We drifted and kissed and talked for a while. Later he told people that had I turned him down, he would have dumped me out of the boat, and swimming is not among my gifts. (I'm about like some dogs or rabbits – I've heard that if an animal has to swim to save his life, he can; but it's not one's preferred means of having a good time.)

The tap-dancing mice and spewing automobile were forgotten. I remember how I kept staring at the ring and gestured excessively to make sure everyone got the point. We have a home movie, now converted to video, of us cavorting at Minnehaha Falls the day after the deed. I'm wearing an unspeakable seventies-style peasant blouse and am red-faced – not from girlish blushing; it was at least ninety that day in vacationland. And I keep flashing The Ring. In that era of delayed marriage and swinging singles, to be proud of being an Engaged Girl seemed a relic of another age, like stockings worn with a garter belt; but I had been very lonely for a very long time and then had wanted to marry this man for a very long time, so there it was. He chased her, she caught him.

Wet pine needles, a scent and a memory. It's been many years since we've been at the lake; the descendants of Tiny and his wife, Orpha, and Harold and his wife, Myrtice, and Charles and Emily Holmquist, who started it all nearly a century ago, now occupy the modernized cottages. Or maybe they're not there anymore. I'm not sure.

But we're still here, Fritz and I. And it is well, I'm now thinking, to recall the urgency and need and inevitability that drove us together, once upon a time—to remember that trembling sense of being players in God's great scheme, and to ponder exactly *why* we wanted to commit our lives to each other.

Today, after the rain, there is sunshine and freshness. My husband has gone to work; my daughter is sleeping late. It is high summer, mid-July, and the cicada's whine has replaced birdsong as the sound rising on the breeze. My suburban world has that "gone fishin' " somnolence that creeps over everything after the Fourth.

In the quiet, I watch flies buzzing on the screen and think about this: Why did I marry him? I could say for companionship, because we shared the same Christian values and goals in life, because I liked the idea of seeing his smile over the Raisin Bran every morning. But those answers, however true—and they are true—sound too dry and itemized. You might as well come up with a cogent answer to the question, Why is summer? Because the sun is on our side of the equator? Because we denizens of the Northland, in places like Chicago and Minnesota, need summer as a respite from winter's gloom?

Summer is because God wills it so, and that is a mystery and delight as large as the morning's storm-washed sky. My marriage is because God likewise wills it so, and it could not be otherwise, and it too is a mystery and a delight. It is at once very small, intimate, even insignificant, *and* a thing of infinite and momentous import.

This, then, is what was birthed on Lake Minnetonka, and actually conceived several years before that, when two people who were somewhat adrift met in a church singles group. And, like a fine vacation day, God has seen that it is good. Clear through.

# *THE ROAD NOT TAKEN (THANK GOODNESS)*

DID YOU EVER LOSE TOUCH with someone who once had been a daily and significant part of your life? Do you ever wonder what happened to them?

The other day I was cleaning out a drawer and came across an old letter from a guy I'll call Gene. Gene and I had been friends years before I met and married Fritz. I haven't heard from him for a long time, and rereading the letter brought no rush of emotion, no torrent of memories—except one. I started thinking about the last time I saw Gene.

It was my first "married summer," and my new husband and I were planning a long driving vacation East. Our itinerary included Boston, where we would see my husband's alma mater and a few old friends, among them Gene. We had kept up an irregular correspondence over the years since he had moved to the East Coast and I knew he now lived in an apartment in Boston. He and Fritz had met once and hit it off, and he invited us to spend a night with him.

My friendship with Gene had fallen into that complicated territory between platonic paldom and romantic commitment. I had never been quite sure what I meant to him, and our paths had diverged before I could find out.

When we arrived at our very expensive hotel in Cambridge (this was years before we became parents and homeowners, and, thus, impoverished), there was a message waiting to call Gene. I did. He was glad to hear from me. After the usual how-was-the-drive-out pleasantries, he informed me that he had recently become interested in astral travel. "I may just float over to your room and say 'How-do,' " he said with a little chuckle.

This was not beginning well.

We arranged for him to pick us up at the hotel later that week, and he would show us the sights and take us back to his apartment. When the morning came, I was waiting in the lobby while Fritz checked us out. I felt a pair of arms around me and there was Gene, newly mustachioed but otherwise looking the same. He brushed me lightly on the cheek and then went, "Hey, there's Fritz!"

Gene drove an orange Rabbit. Called strike one. Erratically, through Boston traffic. He swings and misses. *My* husband drives with the steadiness of the autopilot on a 747.

But he still made me laugh, and he was an informative, entertaining guide as we headed up the road to the country. Then he started telling us about his work, which somehow involved doing stand-up comedy at antinuclear rallies. Radiation humor, anyone? He hits a long foul ball.

At day's end, we returned to Cambridge, where Fritz and I were to pick up our car and our bags and follow Gene's directions to his apartment, which I had assumed was in one of those wonderful tall brick rowhouses. I envisioned hardwood floors, a fireplace, casement windows.

It isn't difficult to get lost in Boston, so when we turned onto a street of decaying, almost tenement-like old apartment houses, I said, "Fritz, I think we've taken a wrong turn."

"This is it," he said.

"Oh. Well, maybe he lives down a few blocks. Let's check the numbers. . . ."

"We're here," he said.

The area was close to being a slum. The streets were littered; threatening-looking individuals lolled around the street corners. It was hot, so hot you could hardly breathe. (So much for fresh sea breezes. I later learned it gets hot in Boston a *lot.*) Maybe Gene had a window unit. Then again.

Gene buzzed us in and hailed us with a hearty greeting from up above. Way up above. Ten steep flights of stairs up above. "I'll help you get your bags up," he said. "These stairs are a bear."

I wanted to scream out, *Gene, you live HERE?*

Well, maybe his place was a well-furnished oasis in this dreadful neighborhood. I had known other people—pastors, for example—who lived, by choice, in shabby parts of town and the interiors of their homes had always been comfortable and tasteful, almost as if to make up for the outer surroundings. And Gene had always had good taste and a certain self-conscious savoir-faire.

The apartment was awful.

Well, maybe more like sad. Gene had fixed up his bedroom (the one with the high-rise view) as the "living" room, with a sofa bed and stereo and other necessities of single-man living. The sole other room was a combination kitchen-dining room, tiled in circa-1928 linoleum and decorated mainly with a Formica-topped table and several chairs. A crowbar rested by the front door, which was equipped with locks that could have served well at Sing Sing.

Gene grinned. He was too smart to say something gratuitous like "Well, what do you think?" but he was pleased to welcome us. And, I reasoned, some people just aren't into ostentation. Maybe Gene was like some social activist who prefers to live at a minimal level of comfort.

We went for dinner at a local Japanese restaurant and talked, and finally, the talk turned real. Gene smiled. Quietly he said, "You know, when I heard you'd gotten married, I have to admit I had a few pangs."

For Gene, closed-in and hard to read, such a statement was tantamount to revelation. The irony was, it didn't matter any more.

I glanced at Fritz, who was beaming. *I won,* the look clearly said. I said something noncommittal like, "Huh!" What do you say when an old friend gives what for him is the closest thing to a declaration of spurned love—in front of your husband?

Later Fritz, gracious in victory, went to bed early (on Gene's sofa bed, in the heat, with no screens on the open windows) while Gene and I talked late. Now that everyone knew where everyone else stood, the tensions of the day had lifted like a wind drives fog away from Boston Harbor. There was a sense of ending, and both Gene and I knew it. He was the past. The man sleeping in the next room was the future.

The next morning Gene stood outside waving as we drove away from the street of tenements, heading for the Mass Pike, on our way to Niagara Falls, where we would spend the night. Fritz honked; I looked back for a long time, then Gene disappeared from view. The rush hour traffic was building—we had to get off to an early start. You see, we had a long road ahead of us.

# *THE DUTCH COWBOY, THE WAR HERO, AND WHAT THEY STARTED*

JACOB NIEUWENHUIJSE was a poor farmer. Unlike the other industrious denizens of his town of Goes, pronounced "Hoos," in the Netherlands, he couldn't coax much out of the rich alluvial soil. He was bored with tending cows. Stories were coming back to the village about America, a place where any man could find work. Jacob was in his twenties, the time a young man should be striking out. He was restless. So he sold his cows, said good-bye to his parents, and set off across the Atlantic in the year of our Lord 1882.

He settled in the Midwest, where he worked as a cowboy and injured his leg falling off a horse. He would walk with a limp the rest of his long life. Later he met and married Katie Hoogerheide, who had also come from the old country, and together they started a grocery store in Kenosha, Wisconsin.

The store prospered. Jacob may have been a poor farmer, but he was a shrewd businessman. He and Katie carefully saved their money, investing it in the stock market. Eventually they were able to send their son Jake – Fritz's dad – to college. Jake wasn't interested in being a shopkeeper. He had dreams of a different sort. Like his father, he was restless and eager to see the world. His college was on the shores of Lake Michigan, north of Chicago, in an area of gracious homes and elm trees that arched across the street. He thought it might be a good place to raise a family someday.

He wasn't quite ready to settle down, however, and spent much of the Great Depression in Hawaii, selling pens. When World War II broke out he enlisted and was sent to Georgia to teach young men how to shoot a rifle.

One of those young men may have been Dick Cody. My dad. "Rich," as his family called him (they pronounced it "Reech," in the small-town Ohio way) had joined up even before the Japanese attacked Pearl Harbor. Like Jake, he had been dissatisfied with the provinces. His father was a charming, not-always-successful businessman who dealt in real estate. The family's fortunes rose and fell with his erratic business. Thank God for Grandma who was energetic and capable and made the best crullers in Miami County. Rich adored her.

Rich wanted to be an artist. He spent many hours in his room, sketching and cartooning. He packed his pens and pads when he was sent overseas and drew and fought his way across France as an officer in the crack Village Fighting Team. He drew evocative, quick sketches of tired infantrymen and smoke rising from ruined cities. Some of them later got published and now are stored in the Library of Congress. He also won a Bronze Star along the way when he led his men across a bridge, in the night, braving enemy fire.

He wanted to forget all that when the war ended and he went to Chicago to look for work with an industrial design firm. A mutual friend introduced him to Beverly Bonfig. The friend told Bev, "There's a really nice guy you should meet. He doesn't know many people in town. . . ."

Bev was intrigued by the intense young artist with the pointed sense of humor. He wasn't like anyone she had ever known. And he kept coming around. They were married in the garden of her parents' estate in the summer of 1946.

Meanwhile, Bette Congdon was a coed at the University of Mississippi when, on a visit to Memphis, a strange officer in uniform hailed her on the street. "Excuse me, Miss, aren't you Bette Congdon from Kenosha?" he asked, with a courteous tip of his cap.

Surprised, she said she was. He had seen a photo of her and recognized her, he explained. She was beautiful, even a little glamorous, with delicate features and big blue eyes. Her looks and charm got her elected Miss Ole Miss, a not inconsiderable honor at the university and an unprecedented accolade for a Yankee.

As they talked, they found they knew a lot of the same people. Jake was her senior by nearly twelve years, an experienced man of the world but with a solid, meat-and-potatoes Midwestern core. He asked if he could call her. She said yes.

And so . . . and so the world turned and turned

again and by the mid-'50s the Codys, including me, were building a house a straight shot down the road from where the Nieuwenhuyses, including Fritz, had built five years before. Old Jacob, now ninety-five and still living in Kenosha, spent most of his time sitting in his chair watching wrestling on TV.

When I was a kid I sometimes wondered what would have happened if my parents hadn't met. Would I still be born to one of them? If so, who? Would I have a personality half me and half someone else? I didn't know, then, about God's sovereignty and timing. They didn't talk much about that in the church I grew up in.

Now I marvel at the confluence of events. *If* Jacob Nieuwenhuijse hadn't been a poor farmer . . . *if* Rich Cody had decided to stay in Miami County . . . and on it goes, season after season, providence after providence. Surely the hand of God is in these things!

I know these stories, because my parents told them to me and Fritz's parents told him and eventually we told each other and now we pass them on to Amanda. They're part of our family lore, an oral tradition in a computerized age. They matter to who we are; they help cement something. When the old tales stop being told, it's time to worry. My hope, therefore, is that someday a mother will be tucking her child in and the child will say, "Mom, tell me again about how Grandpa and Grandma were in a boat and Grandpa asked Grandma to marry him and she couldn't swim very well, so. . . ."

# *WATER BUGS OR BRIEFCASES?*

I SIT AT MY COMPUTER. Staring at it. Agonizing. The right words aren't coming. I look out the window for inspiration but see only a backhoe going by, pulled on a flatbed trailer. Not exactly food for the muse.

For this I quit a good job? This isolation, this struggle? Irregular checks and impatient editors?

My leather briefcase stands in the corner. It's a handsome accessory, a good-bye gift from the company. I've used it exactly twice so far. I hardly ever get out, it seems. Mostly it sits there and gets used as an extra file cabinet.

They really liked me there. I did good work, stayed for years, was a loyal employee. Couldn't beat the benefits, including the intangibles such as office camaraderie and the sense of being significant, a player, in the loop. Most important, I was part of a larger ministry.

Now I'm the ministry, one little person trying to reach the world, or a little piece of it, through my words. And today those words are falling flat. I write a sentence and it thuds lifelessly, instead of dancing.

The four walls begin to close in. I carelessly leave the computer on, burning expensive electricity—Fritz would have a fit—and go get a cup of coffee. Coffee, the writer's stall tactic of choice. Maybe I should call someone. Maybe someone will call me.

Then I hear little feet. Amanda, just out of bed, comes running up to me, smiling, not saying anything. She gives me a hug.

*Now* I remember why I quit.

It's nearly ten in the morning. "Hungry?" I ask, delighted to be freed from the computer, which continues to hum in the next room. Nagging me. I won't come, computer. I have better things to do.

"Is 'Lamb Chop' on?" Lamb Chop is her favorite TV show. Lamb Chop is an adorable puppet, a girl lamb with long eyelashes and curly fleece. I approve of the program; it's sunny and educational and simple fun, no gimmicks or cartoons. I remember Lamb Chop from my childhood.

"Almost," I say, slicing bananas on to cornflakes.

She eats breakfast in front of the TV. Puppeteer Shari Lewis, energetic and ageless, is saying, "Betcha you can't make a '9' out of a '10.' " Then she arranges sticks in certain ways. Pretty cute.

Amanda tells me about her dreams. I pour more juice for her and lounge in the kitchen doorway, listening. I'm happy she's able to sleep late, to linger over breakfast. I want to be the one to cook for her, help her dress, hear her dreams. Time was I had to rush out in the morning while she was still asleep, and her daddy got her up. I got tired of that. He got tired of that. I began to feel, compellingly, as if she needed more of me than she was getting. Or—this may be closer to the truth—I needed more of her than I was getting.

"Aman-da!" A call from across the street. Her fan club awaits. Finished with breakfast and Lamb Chop, she scrambles down and asks me to help her dress. She still lets me help pick her outfits. I like fussing with her long, straight hair. The hair I never had. Headbands, bows, barrettes. A mother acts out her unfulfilled childhood wishes. The bow will be around her neck in short order, I know; but we still try.

"Where will you be?" I ask her.

"Probably over at Megan's."

She's out of here. I tarry awhile, loading the dishwasher, straightening, making beds. The computer is still whirring away in my study. I'd turn it off but that would be admitting defeat. Wish we had stock in the electric company, those highway robbers. Anyway, I'm letting my thoughts simmer, I tell myself.

Back at my station, fiddling with papers. No more excuses. "Getting organized"—stall tactic number thirty-seven. When I worked in an office I had to be efficient, every hour accounted for. Now I have all this time and I twiddle it away.

Or do I? Is welcoming my child in the morning really "twiddling," or something of inestimable importance? And what does my presence at home have to do with my marriage?

A friend of mine once observed that, in his admittedly controversial opinion, a marriage could not tolerate two high-powered careers. "Someone has to be around to tend the relationship," he said. In this age when two paychecks are often needed for basic economic survival, the critical question is, what does it mean to "be around"?

I don't know if my mere physical proximity helps my husband. It's not as if I welcome him home each night dressed in pearls and high heels with a roast bubbling away in the oven. Usually I'm sitting here going, "Hi, wait until I finish this paragraph. Dinner? Um, right." I don't even know if Amanda will respond to my being here most of the time. If anything, she hates it when I play Ideal Mom, hovering and asking her if she wants juice, if she's hot, if she'd like to go for a walk. Get a life, Ma.

My husband too can take care of himself and does. He's a man of the nineties, knows where the laundry hampers are and is capable of turning on the vacuum cleaner. But I know his work takes a toll. I've been there; you don't have a whole lot left when you come home at night. Maybe, then, "tending the relationship" has to do with a certain emotional availability, in not being so preoccupied with your own work and worries that you tune out the needs of others, the way I try to tune out the sounds of the kids playing as I work ("Megan! A water bug! Let's catch it and show it to my mom!").

My working at home is still in the experimental stage. I may keep eyeing that briefcase, picturing it slung chicly over my shoulder as I check in at the departure gate. I may also keep eyeing the undone dishes, unpaid bills, and other things you can escape from when you go out to an office every day.

But I'm going to give it a good, strong try. It's nice, for a change, to hear the voices of children and the chirping of birds instead of chirping phones. It's nice to be there when my daughter and her friends want lemonade. (As we have seen, any and all distractions from HAL the reproachful computer are welcome!) It's nice not to have to give my husband emotional leftovers. I may not be serving up a roast every night, but I am serving up my attention and care.

There's a knock at the back porch door. I turn. Children bearing gifts. They *caught* the water bug.

# *GIVING AWAY THE DOG*

WE HAD TO GIVE AWAY THE DOG.

He was a seventy-five-pound (give or take a few jerks of the leash) Old English Sheepdog. No tail. Lots of hair. One blue eye, one brown. Only a year old, a puppy so big he practically made his own weather. A love of a dog, always ready to jump on you, rub up against you, sit on you in the morning while you were still supine in bed.

But he was too big, too hairy, too much work. Sheep dogs need to be groomed once a month. It's more like owning, say, Secretariat. Ideally, we would prefer a dog who doesn't mind being overlooked, and sheepdogs decidedly mind being overlooked. So the day came when Fritz said, "We have to get rid of him."

"Don't say that," I begged. "At least say, 'We have to find him a new home.' "

So, eventually, we did. He left us several days ago, riding in the back of a Jeep Wagoneer, staring out the back. It was rather sudden; the wife came and said, "I love him; let's try him for a night."

He spent the night in their bedroom, and he didn't come back.

We had had him only six months, but you know how it is with dogs: they take your heart like they grab a Frisbee in their mouths, and they run away with it and you can't get it back. Now (it's funny how you automatically look for dogs) I glance down and don't see anyone. I open a door and brace myself for the furball to bound through, and . . . nothing. No excuse to get exercise. No one pushing his nose through the morning paper to tell us that nature calls and how would *you* like it if you had to wait for someone to take you to the bathroom?

I never thought I would miss him so much.

It's entirely irrational, this man-and-dog thing. Dogs bark annoyingly, slobber, spill their kibble all over the kitchen floor. They're so irritatingly *there* sometimes. They smell—there is nothing like eau de sheepdog after a forced march (his force, my march) in a downpour. A herd of wet alpacas huddled in an Andean stable couldn't smell any worse. But from the time the first maverick wolf crept close to the fire of man and decided he preferred its warmth to the cold of the ceaseless hunt, we have put up with all the dirt and inconvenience.

This is why my daughter and I sat holding each other and sobbing on a night that felt so empty. There is so little that loves you back in this world. Why send something loving away? For his good. For ours.

I write this observing a summer on the downward slope. Now, the night closes in earlier. Already merchants are advertising back-to-school sales. I am making a mental list: Things I want to do with my family before summer ends. The loss of our dog quickens the sense of a time slipping away.

But here is my husband, helping me up!

The day after Ernie (our dog) went away, Saturday, we spent mostly around the house. Wordlessly, we stuck close to each other, a team of two, cleaning and consoling with presence. Amanda, with the resilience of the young, disappeared into play—though, mindful of her loss, we did treat her to a Happy Meal. Knowing, logically, that Fritz was wise in his decision—and that he too was hurting—I did not rail or accuse.

He was here for me, and I for him. And that is the foundational, bedrock strength of marriage: "Someone to help you up." Someone to stand by you when you're feeling lonely and sad and confused. Someone for *you* to help up.

I did not have to tell him how I was feeling. Fourteen years together, that cord of three strands which cannot be broken, teach you to look into the other's heart and do what must be done, unasked, to fill that heart.

Coincidentally, I read just the other day that fewer young people are getting married these days. Too busy with work, they say. Or they haven't met the right person. Or they've seen their own parents' marriages fall apart and they're afraid of committing themselves.

Who will help *them* up when they need it? Their boss? Their jogging buddy? The local barkeep?

Maybe these legions of the assertively alone have been closed up in their office buildings too long to realize it, but seasons do change. Summer slowly moves south. Imperceptibly and inexorably, the slant of light changes from June's high brightness to the mellowness of late August. And one day you wake early in the morning, shivering, and you reach for an extra blanket. Or for the warm body next to you – if there is a warm body next to you.

As for me, I prefer that warm body to be my husband, my man for all seasons. And because of his warmth, his kindness, I am feeling a bit better today. A friend from church, who herself had to give away a beloved dog and was similarly helped up by her husband, dropped by unexpectedly with a gift of homemade strawberry preserves. Ernie's new person called and she too was kind and reassuring. Ernie is happy in his new home. He got a haircut. Their two-year-old wants him to kiss her. They've taken him for many walks. He seems to be eating well, they say.

And now we are talking about another dog, more inconvenience. We have a dream of a fuzzy-haired mutt with floppy ears and a raggedy mutt tail, always wagging, and smiling brown eyes. He will be about the color of whole-wheat toast. We're thinking of naming him Harvey.

You can have a lot of fun with a dog in the fall, you know. There are still a lot of warm days left. And we both need the exercise.

# *FALL*

# *ROUND AND ROUND SHE GOES...*

EVER HAD A PICNIC in a supermarket parking lot?

I never had either, until last Wednesday night. It was one of those evenings when everything backs into everything else and something has to give – in this case, dinner at home. See, we had to go to the grocery store. We were down to eating spaghetti with leftover gravy, so it was time; but we couldn't go until Fritz came home from work. Then we had to rush Amanda to her church club, after which I was due at a friend's house for a quick visit. Bing bing bing.

Newenhuyse's Law: "Everything always takes more time than you think it will." By the time we got out of the supermarket we had seven minutes to get to church. So there I stood in the parking lot, making sandwiches on the car hood with the turkey bologna and bread we had purchased. The sunset, which volcanic ash had turned into a rosy spectacle, was fading rapidly. (It's something about the sulfur crystals reflecting the light.) I shoved one at Amanda. "Here! Eat!" Grabbed a raw carrot out of its plastic bag. Found some yogurt for Fritz (we had, with wonderful foresight, brought along spoons). Fritz drove practically no-handed as he ate. Amanda somehow found the cookies we had bought and ate a half-dozen.

Somehow we made it to church on time. The bag of bread lay opened on the car floor because I couldn't find the twist tie in the dark. Amanda had strewn bologna rind around. But we were on time.

Then it was off to Charlotte's. I thought I remembered where she lived, but we couldn't find it in the dark and overshot the street. Newenhuyse's Law, Part two: "Never trust your short-term memory past forty." Then the road was torn up in front of her house and we couldn't figure out how to get across. By now we were bickering, in the way couples do when they've been driving around in circles for a half-hour. When I finally knocked, she didn't answer and I had to go around to the back and stand on the deck and pound on the back sliding door while peering into the kitchen. I'm glad no neighbor saw.

Later, back in the car, Amanda was chattering and bouncing up and down. "What's she been eating?" I asked Fritz suspiciously. "Six Twixes," he replied. Then he volunteered that he reckoned he'd been driving for almost two hours straight.

Home. Scrape out the food remains from the car—what we can see; the rest will have to fester in there until daylight. Finish putting away groceries. Hear about club. They're going to have a cookout next week and make S'mores. Amanda will have to wear a mask, but it's NOT a Halloween party. They call one teenage helper "Aunt Mike." "Don't you think he'd get a complex?" Fritz muses.

Slowly the evening wound down and caught its breath. Eventually, a family slept.

The next day was similar. Up before dawn to finish an article that HAD to get in. Deliver article. Visit around former office. A doctor's appointment. Buy produce at the Farmer's Market. Pick up Amanda for lunch. Come home and there are three messages on the machine. Deal with messages. Prepare for a dinner meeting. Go to dinner meeting.

This is how it's been around here lately. I feel like we're on this mad carousel, *careering* from one thing to the next, instead of moving slowly and with intention. And it's mostly little stuff, but pile it all together and it creates a rather formidable mountain of busyness. A friend gives us his swing set and he and Fritz spend all one Saturday morning wrestling it up. We have to buy a wedding gift. There's a supper at church with visiting missionaries. People come to the door selling things. We take care of my mother's dogs for a while.

And we eventually come to a day when we HAVE to do laundry and clean the house, especially the space, too small for a vacuum or an adult-sized hand, between Amanda's bed and nightstand that we call "the dungeon" because things disappear down there, never to be seen again—including, I fear, some foodstuffs.

Maybe it's the fall, with everything revving up. Maybe it's my career change—when I left the office, I thought we were "downscaling." Instead I've substituted eight things for one thing. Some downscaling. Maybe it's Amanda getting older and having more going on. Maybe it's my good-Christian-girl inability to say no to hospitality, work, volunteer help. Maybe it's just life in the suburbs.

Whatever, it's been a very long time since we got up with a free day stretching before us, a day to sit around and say, "What shall we do on this beautiful morning?" Even if the rain was pouring down, it would be beautiful if we had free time. Even if that time was simply spent reading the newspaper together (yes, even Amanda), or going for a walk (yes, even in the rain), it would be beautiful.

This is what you miss when life gets hectic: the feeling that you're living *thoroughly.* I really like the pot of chrysanthemums we got for our front steps. It's a big bouquet, burnt-orange powder puffs. We always rush right by it, and that bothers me sometimes. I like having time to read a magazine straight through, time to call my sister-in-law in California, just to say "How ya doin'?" Even time to straighten the towels in the linen closet. I get tired of the feeling that we're always cutting corners, doing the minimum as we run to catch up with our schedule.

We talk about this a lot. "Wouldn't it be nice to spend Sunday afternoon driving through small towns out in the country?" Fritz suggested yesterday. Yes, but how? Amanda may have children's choir practice. I may have to finish a chapter. He'll be driving back from a wedding he's giving.

What about a weekend spiritual retreat? And wouldn't it be nice to, someday, take a real sabbatical? Rent a house in Vermont for a summer or something? I wonder if foundations give grants to burned-out couples. Here's $50,000. Go have fun with it!

In your dreams, kiddo.

In a way, it's nice to be this busy, this wanted. All these connections are satisfying and stimulating for our marriage. There have been times when we haven't been very busy or very wanted, when we were mostly thrown on our own resources, two against the world, and it was a lonely feeling indeed. Still, there's got to be a balance in there somewhere, a state of equilibrium halfway between boring and crazy. You can't stop the machine entirely, but maybe you can turn down the motor a notch.

Until we find that paradisical state, I guess we'll keep careering around, grabbing for those brief moments of respite as they come along. And, maybe, as long as we're keeping each other steady on the merry-go-round, and as long as we're able to hear each other's voices above the whir of the gears, it will be enough. But we'll be sure to have directions.

# *MR. FIXIT AND THE TRUCK-DRIVING ANGEL*

"BETSEY! GET UP!"

A strange male voice? At seven in the morning? There was a flurry of knocking on the bedroom door, then it cracked open. I dived under the covers and heard a familiar hoot of laughter as the door slammed. Who else but Tom? Lanky, red-haired Tom, here early to fix something. He and Fritz thought it was really funny. Guy humor at its scintillating best. "Hi, Tom," I called out. " 'Bye, Tom."

Tom comes over a lot, showing up at odd hours or when it's raining. He's our handyman, on a seemingly permanent retainer. I tease him that we should file adoption papers on him, he's around so much. Whether it's a leaky pipe in the basement or a door off its hinges or new cabinet handles, Tom can fix it. No job too small.

That's not all Tom does. Once Tom was here for some job and I was having computer problems. Tom spent a long time on the phone, trying to track down repair people for us. He drove home to fetch a monitor and brought it back. It didn't work, but that was all right. We'll forgive Tom a lot.

Tom likes to give Fritz a hard time: "Whatcha been doing, Fritz, putting your fist through the door? C'mon, get over here and give me a hand!" Fritz gives it right back. Tom puts him to work, but never makes Fritz feel inadequate because he isn't the handyman some guys are. For most of the summer he was building an addition not far from us, and he would often rattle by our house in his van and yell something out as he did so.

Tom's a Christian too; goes to our church, where he's Mr. Everything. Tom's a good friend. He even bought wrapping paper from Amanda. He didn't have to, but that's how Tom is. Kind of like the uncle everybody wished they had.

Yesterday Fritz and I were eating lunch when

the doorbell rang. Figuring it was the mail carrier, he answered the door. It was our friend Charlene, wanting to take me to lunch. "Even if you've already eaten, come with me," she said. "I'm hungry." She and Fritz talked about books and faith while I got ready. We went to Taco Bell and Charlene got a very wan-looking tostada. "This isn't like any tostada I've ever seen," she said, trying unsuccessfully to eat it with her fingers. I laughed. Charlene, as usual, got right to the heart of the matter. She had interviewed a woman for a newspaper article—Charlene's a writer—and the woman had struck her as overly driven, even sacrificing her family in the pursuit of a glamorous career. "But then, how can we judge?" she said between mouthfuls of the impostor tostada. "Who am I to say she shouldn't pursue a dream? Gee, Bets, it's complicated."

Tom and Fritz josh. Charlene and I get down to brass tacks.

This isn't the first time she has dropped by unexpectedly. Once I was walking to school to pick up Amanda, in one of my periodic black moods when I feel like a lint ball on the carpet of life, when a white truck pulled up. I didn't recognize the truck, wasn't in the mood to give directions and kept slumping along. "Going my way?" she yelled. We drove Amanda home and, since Fritz wasn't working that day, she took me out for a respite. "You were like an angel coming along just then," I told her at the restaurant. "An angel in a white truck."

Charlene gives me what I need, an open heart and listening ear and honest, hard-won wisdom. Tom gives Fritz what he needs, a man to work alongside and enjoy companionship with. I like Tom and Fritz likes Charlene. Both friendships are immeasurably dear and valuable. They're more like the ideal extended family, the way they drop in. These and other friendships keep my husband and me from falling back on each other too much. The day I was in my pit, I couldn't burden my husband. He had a lot on his mind and I needed a fellow writer to talk to. Fritz, for his part, needs a sort of rough camaraderie that I don't understand. I need to be face-to-face with a friend. He prefers being elbow to elbow, working on something together.

There are others. Tyrone, who painted our kitchen (elbow to elbow) and told Fritz about growing up on Chicago's West Side and being forced to drop out of college because the family didn't have the money. Lou, Fritz's occasional prayer partner. The people Fritz works with. The people I used to work with and still count as friends. Practical Louise, who schedules me for bimonthly lunches and helps solve my problems even though she's ten years younger. Curtis, who qualifies as "family friend." Even Amanda's friend Danielle, who's around here so much I sometimes feel like her aunt. She's a bright, interesting little girl.

This is one thing I like about our family of friendships: I know his friends and he knows mine, and many of them are "our" friends. We talk about them and we're most thankful for them. In fact, so strong are our connections to many of these people that we would have to think long and hard before moving.

Connections strengthen a marriage. *Community,* the sense of being rooted in a particular environment, strengthens a marriage. You know other people are thinking of you, praying for you, pulling for you. They can step in when you need help. They give you more to talk about; they add texture to your life. Friends even help you to be independent of each other. If I want to go see a genteel British movie that I know my husband wouldn't particularly enjoy, I can round up a group of friends for girls' night out. Or he can arrange to go to the high-school football playoffs with another guy (preferably with one of them holding a wrench so they feel more at ease).

Husbands and wives, of course, approach friendships differently. I encourage (read: push) Fritz to get out. "Go to the men's breakfast at church!" I said to him today. He hedged and said probably, although we're also going to a wedding that day and one social event may use up his quota. I, of course, need no such encouragement; if anything, he thinks I talk too long on the phone (men's phone conversation: "Hello? Oh, hi. Yeah, OK. 'Bye."). I always have my feelers out for new people to know; Fritz tends to stumble on to friendships.

That's all right. Two social butterflies in one family (make that three; my daughter takes after me in her pursuit of peers) would be an infestation.

All this has taken a long time—eight years of living in this town. When we first moved here we could hardly put together a Christmas-card list beyond relatives and the same college friends we've been exchanging cards with forever. Now we send out as many as the mayor of a small city. The postage costs more than some of our gifts. Yet we wouldn't omit anyone.

Fritz and I are best friends, and I don't say that glibly. We truly enjoy one another's company. But I think part of the reason we get along so well is because of people like Tom and Charlene. Tom says, "Do chores for your wife!" Charlene says, "Make a big deal of his birthday!" They care for us—and our marriage—and in doing so, help us care for each other. So I guess I'll tolerate Tom's periodic reveilles. But that hooting. . . .

# *TREASURES ON EARTH; OR, HOW YOUR STUFF CAN HURT YOU*

"DEAR? COULD YOU GET A PAN OUT for me?"

Of course I could get it myself. I am able-bodied, after a fashion. But the ensuing action will show you why I cannot.

My husband crouches down on his hands and knees. "Which one did you want?"

"The dark-brown saucepan, for cooking rice."

Clang! Clatter! Skillets and stockpots and mismatched lids come cascading out of the cupboard in a utensil rockslide. My husband bites his lip, trying to keep his language suitable for family consumption. "Aauugghh!" he bellows.

An iron frying pan, so old it was probably forged by Longfellow's village smithy, has fallen onto his pinky. He runs cold water on the throbbing digit. "We've got to do something about that cabinet."

Now you see why I have him do this. I have him put away pans too because when I do it I hurry and stuff them in helter-skelter and slam the door as fast as I can—with predictable results once the cupboard is open. My husband is a patient man, but even he has his limits. When your own things start hurting you, it's time to take a stand.

And the pan cabinet is now so full the hinge is coming off and the middle shelf is listing at a dangerous angle. One day the whole thing will collapse and we will have to leave everything out, just sitting visibly on the counter.

"Fritz," I say. "We have too many pans."

"I know," he agrees.

"We have too many things," I go on, stroking his finger. "Too many tapes, too many clothes, too many books, multiples of everything. We have more stuff than my mother and she's lived in her house thirty-seven years. We've GOT to do something."

Then he spoke the words I've been dreading: "We have to have a garage sale."

Again.

We had a garage sale just a year ago, in mid-autumn. My mother-in-law, who has been a major player in her church's rummage sale since the Russians launched Sputnik, came and helped with sorting and display and customer service. The merchandise filled not only the garage, but the driveway and the backyard. Our property looked like a Middle Eastern *souk.* I'm surprised our town's zoning board didn't slap us with some violation. We had so much stuff that tagging each individual item was impossible. Instead we made up a price list on a big piece of poster board. Everything must go!

And it did.

"If you sell it, they will come," I said to Fritz later. Russian immigrants rubbed shoulders with retired grandpas and poor students and those serious yard-sale habitues you can spot a mile away. People of all tongues and races pawed through our unwanted excess and happily took it off our hands and out of our lives.

Afterward we stood around feeling lightheaded and junk-free, almost cleansed. We had netted about $250 in the form of small bills and loose change. The garage looked as empty as a monk's cell; the basement was navigable. Here was a fresh start!

Or so we thought. But here the year has come full circle to another fall. The frost is on the pumpkin, the birds are on the wing . . . and we *need* another garage sale, because our things are out of control. They're exploding exponentially, like an especially fertile colony of voles.

How did this happen? And why have things, anyway?

Here is one reason. When it comes to garage sales, my mate taketh away as well as giveth. He isn't quite as fanatic as those devotees who arm themselves with pocket street guides, routes highlighted in yellow, and slowly drive around in pairs, stopping at all the sales advertised in the local rag that week.

A parenthetical anecdote here: Some people are really over the top in their fanaticism. One spring Saturday morning I was alone in the house, in the bathroom, when the doorbell chimed. As I was still in my robe I was tempted not to answer, but I was curious. There on the front porch stood a strange older man. "Aren't you having a garage sale?" he demanded, in a tone that implied we *should* be having one if we were any kind of real Americans. "Um, no," I said. "Well, I know there's one right around here," he said, making no move to leave.

This was getting downright threatening. "Well, I can't help you!" I returned curtly and slammed the door.

Then there's Lois, Fritz's second cousin who's actually more like an aunt. Lois doesn't need a map or a classified section. She has a built-in detector for garage sales—and Goodwill stores—and church bazaars. Lois will be driving home from shopping, when suddenly she will veer quickly off the main drag. "Yard sale," she says. How she knew, I have no idea, but there it is, pennants shining in the San Fernando Valley smog. If it's gently used, secondhand, fragrant with the must of the years, Cousin Lois will scent it out.

They say blood will tell, and apparently my man has inherited some Holmquist gene for bargaining and acquiring. On Saturday mornings, if he goes to the bank or off to play basketball in the church league, I know not to expect him before noon because he'll be out hunting and gathering, returning with his booty of children's clothes, recordings by obscure Christian rock groups and coffee mugs that say things like "I am a working woman. I am nuts" on them. Or maybe he'll be toting an enormous, moth-eaten Garfield ("think Amanda would like this?" "I . . . want . . . that . . . OUT!").

The problem is, where is "out"? Out is into the garbage, at the cost of a dollar per large item, or into the garage (note that only one letter separates "garage" from "garbage"), or down to the basement. Which my husband views as a sort of holding pen for junk he eventually plans to pass on to the poor people. Somehow. "It's a shame to throw these things away," he always says. "Someone could use it."

"Poor people need jobs, education, access to decent health care," I shoot back. "Not five-foot Garfields. Besides, junk is not a terrible thing to waste."

"But what about the landfill crisis? You know they're filling up. . . ."

The argument from environmentalism. No wonder I throw up my hands and give in.

But I must be fair. It isn't all Bargain-o-mania that's responsible for our critical mass. I think there's some physical law of matter expansion governing our accretions. Things breed, accumulate, enlarge, or just kind of drift in from the outside, to squat here permanently. Someone gives you a cheese tray, or a set of socket wrenches, that you know you won't ever use. Were I ruthless and efficient, I would give the thing away posthaste, take it to the local resale shop. But inertia and sentiment—a deadly combination when one is trying to de-thing one's living quarters—set in. It seems rude to just junk a well-intentioned gift. So the stuff gets put away somewhere, and the result, as we have seen, is the black hole of accumulation: our stuff has expanded so much that it collapses upon itself and tries to suck us in with it. THAT'S why the iron skillet hit Fritz. It was trying to *take* him.

That incident was, indeed, a watershed, the Concord Bridge, Fort Sumter, Pearl Harbor of our battle against things. Never again. We're going to soldier on with our garage sale. We'll hold it in the sleet if we have to (but remember, they will come). I want everything out of here before Christmas. Permanent vacation and all that. Free at last.

Then why do I feel like somewhere a giant Garfield doll, stashed away in an unknown attic, is smirking, "Oh, yeah?"

# *COMING HOME*

*I WISH I HADN'T AGREED TO THIS,* I thought. My back and neck were starting to ache. My feet hurt. I wanted a cup of coffee. I was bored. I had a million things to do and here I was, standing in the hallway at my daughter's school, collating the weekly newsletter and feeling deeply sorry for myself. Across the hall the gym teacher was encouraging her class, "I don't care if you win! Just try! Show some spirit!"

Twenty-three, twenty-four, twenty-five, hit the electric stapler . . . show some spirit. *Boy, am I tired. Why do I not learn how to say no?* When I had signed up for this I had expected we would be a convivial group of moms working together for the good of Hawthorne Elementary School. Instead, here I was. Alone. Ignored. Doing tasks a chimpanzee or robot could be taught to perform. I wanted to cry.

Finally I was done. Now I had to trudge home. The autumn afternoon was gorgeous, an ash tree had turned and the butterflies were heading south, but I hardly noticed. All I could think about was getting home and getting some rest. And I wanted my husband.

It had not been one of my better weeks. Computer problems, some of them a result of my own mechanical obtuseness, had kept me from writing. I had been stung by a bumblebee—twice—in my own kitchen—and my hand had swollen up in reaction. And my husband had started a new job and was working longer hours, with less flexibility than we had enjoyed before.

That was it. I really missed him.

When I got home the messages were piled up on the answering machine. A UPS package had arrived, a manuscript I needed to read. I would deal with them later. Right now I had to take a nap. I threw myself on the unmade bed . . .

. . . and woke an hour later, feeling better.

Now it was time to get ready for my beloved to come home. I couldn't let him return to a messy house and no dinner prepared. Feeling like a 1950s wife, I bustled around defrosting a chicken, washing the dishes, feeding the parakeets, making the beds, straightening the house. In the mail a postcard had come from a childhood playmate of Fritz's. I would surprise him with it.

My daughter had come home from school. I admired her schoolwork, fixed her some popcorn, and agreed to buy some overpriced wrapping paper she was selling for a fundraiser.

By now it was nearly 5. He would be home in a few minutes. Better walk the dogs real quick. Down the street with them, mission accomplished, return home—and there he was, pulling into the garage!

My husband, my heart, my home. I couldn't believe I could still feel like this after fourteen years.

He was carrying grocery sacks. "Guess what? I got dinner," he said after kissing me. "I figured you wouldn't want to cook after your hard day."

What a man! We embraced again, right out in public. Let 'em look.

*This is what makes it work,* I thought. He thinks of me; I think of him.

We went into the kitchen and unloaded the groceries. I told him about my horrible day; he shared the events at work. "I've MISSED you," I said honestly.

And I had.

After Cokes were poured we went into the living room to unwind. Amanda was out playing; the weather had turned crisp after a week of hanging mugginess and thunder; I had finally resolved my computer situation and I didn't have to collate any more newsletters. We agreed that maybe I should tender my resignation from that key position. I showed him the postcard. "Bill Quigley!" he said in amazement.

We talked, briefly, about old times and old ties. Mainly I just enjoyed his company—and felt my emotional tank filling up. I knew he was feeling the same way.

"This is nice," I sighed.

Revelation, again: No one can do what a spouse does. Through this trying week I had whined to several friends and they had been appropriately solicitous. I had showed all comers my bee-stung hand, told the story of the mishap over and over and with increasing relish, and had received sympathy and medical advice. The phone kept ringing with work opportunities. But all fell away before the primacy of this one man, this one relationship.

The force of my need surprised me. I had always been independent, overbusy, one to preach the necessity for connections outside the marriage. And here I was, like a twenty-two-year-old whose fiancé had come home on leave from the service!

*It is not good for man or woman to be alone. . . .*

As dear as my friends are, as stimulating as my writing contacts are, I am not the most important person in their lives. I cannot go to them time and time again and expect attention and succor; I would do so with guilt and apologies. I do not, however, have to apologize to my husband for needing him. He's on my side, on my team. And I am on his. We reach out our hands for each other's consolation, presence, perspective.

Here is the tragedy of a marriage gone bad: when you reach out and the other turns away expressionless. I cannot imagine a more abysmal desolation, an emotional homelessness, short of separation from God Himself. Where do you go to get out of the cold?

Walking from school that day, I was intent on home, a place to go, a bed to fall on. I was, really, intent on my husband and thinking about the encircling welcome I would eventually receive from him, who is there when everything else falls away.

The sun was going down. Amanda came in, having found at least one customer for wrapping paper. Time to eat. We turned on some lights and closed a few windows against the cold.

# *ECHOES OF THE BELLS*

NINETEEN SEVENTY-EIGHT.

*Saturday Night Fever* and the Bee Gees. Farrah Fawcett hair and the Jonestown massacre. Platform shoes and Proposition 13. Blizzards in Boston and Chicago. And a wedding.

In a church ladies' lounge/powder room, a bride prepares. She puts the finishing touches on her blush, lip gloss, eye makeup. Her hair, brushed back in wings, smells like the beauty salon she came from this morning. She surveys herself critically in the mirror from all angles. This fluorescent light makes her skin look mottled. She is in a dream world. . . .

"Betsey! Everyone's waiting! It's 4:30!"

Well, what bride wears a watch?

Her sister and matron of honor has come to corral her. *Her* hair is curled like Sally Struthers' in "All in the Family" and she wears tinted glasses. A generation, living down the styles of its '70s nuptials.

"You look fine. Here, fix your collar. Take your flowers. Let's go!"

Slowly the bride ascends the stairs to the church vestibule, holding her long skirts so as not to trip. She cannot believe this is happening. Then she hears the music of the prelude, hymns of the season she and her fiancé requested, like "We Gather Together." They scheduled the wedding for Thanksgiving weekend to make it easier for out-of-town guests to join them. She sees heads turning, necks craning as the organist strikes up "Jesu, Joy of Man's Desiring." She *knows* these people. Every face is familiar. They're here for her.

Oh, dear.

Her sisters process down the aisle, looking richly autumnal in shades of violet and lavender. Here's her dad, handsome and serious in a dark suit. It's time.

"Trumpet Voluntary" is the signal for the bride. They rehearsed all this last night. Then, she felt confident. Now, with everyone standing and smiling at her, she feels her legs turn to mush. She grips her father's arm; if he weren't there she would collapse in a satin heap on the floor. The bride wore bruises.

Her cheeks are flaming. Now she knows where the term "blushing bride" came from. One, stop. Two, stop.

There he is, smiling at her from the chancel steps. Not smiling. *Beaming.*

She fixes her eyes on his face. His smile is the lighthouse beacon urging her on. Fortunately the chapel is small, the aisle short.

"Dearly beloved. . . ."

Who gives this woman? Her dad has practiced his part over and over: "Her mother and I do." He takes his seat, the ancient transfer having been made.

Something that matters greatly, a disturbance in the universe, is going on here. The sanctuary is hushed. From somewhere she hears a sniff. "Submit to one another out of reverence for Christ. . . ."

She loves the idea of serving each other. Someday she will find out what that really means. She looks at the minister, then at the man who in minutes will be her husband. As in other momentous times of her life, she feels dreamlike, unreal. Like she's watching herself get married, and the real person is peeping through a side door observing all this.

The vows. This is it. Her voice trembles a bit: "I, Elizabeth, take thee, Frederick. . . ."

Now the ring. Let's see. Hand her sister the bouquet. What if there's been a slipup and he doesn't have the ring? You hear about these things. But he has the ring, and he slips it on her finger, and it glistens.

"I now pronounce you husband and wife." A gentle kiss, a murmur from the assemblage. She feels herself starting to relax. Mendelssohn peals out from the pipe organ. Her dad says, audibly, "I'll be!" and everyone laughs.

She floats through the reception, held in the church social room, a lovely space with carpeting, tall Georgian windows, a working fireplace, comfortable armchairs for guests like her husband's grandmother, who holds court in one corner, wearing a fur stole. She has asked a professional acquaintance from downtown to take photos, candid shots using available light. Nothing intrusive, no endless lining up of the wedding party while guests wait impatiently. Catered hors d'oeuvres, punch, cake. A string quartet, friends of her teenage sister, play by the fireplace. They wanted to celebrate here, in the church where they met.

Quite a bit later, she leaves her girlhood home forever, in a hail of rice. The relatives have adjourned there to kick off their shoes and eat a late supper of cold cuts and salads; she, however, is heading downtown with her husband, to a honeymoon weekend at Chicago's Drake Hotel, where royalty stay. The car has been decorated with shaving cream: JUST MARRIED. The two of them honk and wave their way down Lake Shore Drive, feeling giddy, tired, and very newly wedded.

They have a choice room with a lake view. Sofas by the window. A gift basket of fruit. Too busy to eat much at her own wedding, she peels a banana and munches. They sink down on the sofas and look at each other. . . .

Every so often we like to get our wedding album

out from the living-room cabinet and look at it. The white binding now has patches of green fuzz on it; something stuck to it once, probably during a move when it was piled in a box of books. The color photos have faded, taking on a golden hue. The wedding, in memory, probably has too. Still, it's fun to reminisce, especially with Amanda: Did I really wear my hair like that, so stiff and blown back? Look at the men's sideburns! Who's that, Mom? Someone I haven't heard from in years, but their legacy lives on in the form of those orange and brown dishtowels, now in the rag drawer. Why wasn't *I* there? Because God hadn't thought of you yet.

It was a lovely wedding, a personal wedding. Even the time, November, was handpicked, off the pattern; I don't know anyone else who was married in November. The name itself signals a dreariness. But that day the sun shone!

So what difference does a wedding make? Isn't it just a public ceremony that affirms a commitment a man and a woman have already privately made? Couldn't you get married just as well out in the woods, say, "I marry you," three times or something, and it would have just as much meaning? And what about all the weddings where the strains of Mendelssohn are drowned out by the judge's gavel and the divorce decree?

Well, I'm not so sure a wedding is just meaningless pomp. I think about our wedding every time our anniversary rolls around. We began among friends, surrounded by beauty and hope and faith (there were four or five minister friends among the guests). We were *launched,* and the echoes resonate still.

It's important, those evenings when you haven't much to say to each other (and we all do have those times, you know), to listen for those echoes, the ringing of the bells. No matter how many years it's been, if you prick up the ears of your soul—you will hear them.

# *TO A YOUNG BRIDE*

WELL, MICHELLE, it was a beautiful wedding. The bagpipes at the end were a special touch, as were the vows you and Andy wrote yourselves. It was fun seeing so many old friends. Even the wedding cake was good—cheesecake! Great touch!

Now you and Andy are off to Massachusetts and your new life. He'll be getting a taste of life in the pastorate. So will you. Hard road; but you both love the Lord, and I know He'll be with you. But in a way, I envy you, you know. So much ahead of you—work, building a home, babies eventually. So much to learn.

We gave you a wedding gift, but I'd like to pass on some words from an old married lady that might help you as you and Andy begin. . . .

*Give in.* I suspect, Michelle, that you're as strong-minded as I am. Life has pretty much broken your way so far. You're intelligent, independent, and you've come of age in an era when many young people expect to remain autonomous and independent once they're married. Some women don't even change their names. I understand those desires; my generation was the first to struggle with all this, not always successfully.

But an insistence on selfhood, on fifty-fifty, on equality at all costs, can be wearying and destructive of God's idea for two-become-one. There will be times when you and Andy don't agree on something. There will be times when you're both tired after work and neither of you will want to cook or run errands. Try being the one to say, "OK, we'll do it your way"; or "You take it easy. I'll make dinner."

I'm not talking about a distorted view of submission. I am talking about serving each other, about inconveniencing yourself for the sake of the other—as Christ did for us. And I would give Andy the same advice.

*Check in with each other.* It's easy to let careers

and children and chores come between you and your spouse. You may not believe this now, but trust me, it happens to all of us. Life gets hectic, the calendar gets crowded, your mind gets overfull, and one evening you stop short and realize you've hardly spoken to your spouse all day except to remind him you have a meeting tonight. Activity is a good thing; every marriage needs outside stimulation. And you may not always be able to set aside an hour each day, just for the other. But *remember* your spouse. Don't let too much time go by before you have that hour.

*Know what true fidelity means.* We Christians can place such an emphasis on sexual fidelity that we forget there are other, subtler, ways to stray. I think that for women, sexual temptation is less of an issue than it is for men. The things that tempt us are different. A too-close *emotional* connection with another man. Confiding in our female friends rather than sharing with our husband. Pouring ourselves into our children and not giving the same intensity to the marriage relationship. Becoming so absorbed in our career that our marriage gets pushed down from being number one.

This happens in part because kids, friends, work have the element of novelty. They're interesting, always changing. Our spouse is always there, the constant backdrop to the action. Don't let him become the backdrop, though! Share your world with him. Ask him his opinion. And please . . . pray for him, regularly and throughout the day. I remember once my husband was facing a particularly tough day at work. He *had* to get certain projects accomplished. All that day I was sending up arrow prayers: "Lord, please help Fritz with. . . ." It worked!

*Remember the critical role of a larger community of caring.* In the beginning you may be moving around a fair amount, so this may not be easy. But a circle of friends, a good church, the support of extended family are invaluable props to a marriage. I may even go so far as to say that there are times when this "community" can make the difference between a marriage that thrives and a marriage that languishes, dry and unnurtured. People live in such isolation these days, lonely little nuclear families forced to rely on their own resources. It isn't healthy. If you must live away from extended family, find another kind of "family." Seek out the advice of wise older Christians. Celebrate holidays with friends. Maybe find a prayer partner. We need each other!

*Talk . . . and talk some more.* The beauty of talking is that it's convenient, you can do it anywhere, and it doesn't cost anything. Talk in the car, talk in bed, talk on the phone, talk while you work around the house, talk over morning coffee. It's less important what you talk *about* than that you're communicating. Don't artificially force the issue: "It's time to communicate!" (Besides, if your husband is like most men, including my husband, he'll wonder what he's done wrong if you take that approach.) Talk about your childhoods, about the news, about incidents at work, about your favorite foods, about books . . . whatever. It's the greatest glue for intimacy there is. Well, the second greatest.

*Learn from one another.* When I got married I thought my husband and I were exactly alike, male and female versions of the same soul, almost like long-lost brother and sister. And we are a lot alike; we're not opposites like some couples I know. But we're also a lot different. So are you two, and you probably know that already. But God has put the two of you together for many reasons, and one of them is to *complete* the other. For example, my husband is more phlegmatic than I am. His calm, his avoidance of conflict can frustrate me. He's Dutch, I'm Irish—get the picture? But I realize that his serenity and rational approach are just what I need. He holds me down, gives me perspective. Likewise, I energize him, help open him up. It's a good combination.

*And when the going gets tough* . . . Michelle, if I know your dad, he has already enlightened you to the fact that sometimes really terrible things happen. Money troubles. Kid troubles. Illness. Loss of a job. I pray your life will be sunny and flower-filled, but I have a feeling there'll be thorns along the way too. This is when you stop talking, stop analyzing, stop negotiating. This is when you put your arms around your spouse and silently say, I'm here. We're in this together. God will get us through. He needs you right now, and you need him. Be each other's shelter. Cry together. Even make black-humor jokes together. See God's face together.

You are each other's bottom line, final word, bedrock foundation. You begin your life with the most important part of that foundation already laid: Jesus Christ. Build on that, and you will have created a structure to last a lifetime.

# *CHEZ WAL-MART AND OTHER FAVORED GETAWAYS*

"WE HAVE TO CELEBRATE our tenth anniversary," I said to my husband. "Do a getaway weekend."

"We have no money," he responded.

"We have a little. And you can't put a price tag on renewing your marriage, they say. Besides, Bolinders went to *Alaska* on their fifteenth. Everyone does it up big for these special occasions. Listen, I saw this ad in the paper. Special weekend rates. . . ."

The Mayfair Regent was delighted to accommodate us. The Mayfair Regent is a European-style small hostelry on a one-block street that ends at the lake. Afternoon tea is served in the lobby. The only hotel restaurant is a French place at the top of the hotel. There is no coffee shop. No one to shine your shoes or style your hair. No phalanxes of bellpersons wait around the bell desk, ready to take your bags and your money. This is not your father's Hilton. (We stayed at a Hilton once during a convention. And, even though we arrived with this incredibly tacky pile of junk stuffed in plastic supermarket bags—plus a big box of diapers—the all-American bell staff treated our bags as if they were Hermes, and us as if we were friends.)

This, however was *Continental.* And Continental people are smaller than Americans. They live in little apartments or rowhouses, packed together with other small people. They drive small cars or ride small bicycles to small stores on narrow streets. Therefore, I should not have been surprised when the single bellperson opened the door to our room. The bed occupied most of the space. There was one armchair, one armoire, a tiny writing desk. The windows, tall and narrow, reminded me of the openings—I think they're called barbicans—twelfth-century bowmen would shoot arrows through in defending their castle.

"Where's the TV?" wondered Fritz, who, though he went to an Ivy League school and has traversed the glittering capitals of Europe, is essentially a heartland kind of guy. You can take the boy out of the Midwest, but you can't take the Midwest out of the boy.

The bellman, with the air of a pastry chef unveiling a creation of a spun-sugar swan, threw open the door of the armoire. There the TV sat. In a Continental *pension,* it does not do to have its twenty-five-inch eye staring at you. So it has to sulk behind mahogany doors.

Oddly, the bathroom (or do you say lavatory?) was about the same size as the bedroom, complete with a white robe hanging on the door. "Maybe this is complimentary, like the shampoo," said my beloved. I admired the basket of soaps. We don't get out much, you know.

The bellperson was still sort of milling about by the door. I elbowed Fritz, who gauchely overtipped. The man looked at us with that half-condescending, half-servile gaze peculiar to those in the employ of finer hotels, and left.

"Well. Here we are," I said, claiming the chair.

"Ten years," Fritz said. "How about that. Boy." He drifted over to the barbican and gazed out as if watching for marauding Moors. Just then the phone rang. A Continental-accented voice informed us that a basket of fruit was on its way up to our room, compliments of the management.

The fruit *was* delicious. It was so delicious that by the time we went down for afternoon tea we were full and could manage only a couple of scones and a bit of the tea, which was an exotic brew from someplace like the Seychelles or maybe New Jersey. Truth to tell, neither of us even likes tea very much. But you're supposed to have tea at the Mayfair, so that is what we did.

"Now what do you want to do?" asked Fritz.

"I don't know," I said, feeling about as energetic as a slug. "Go for a walk? That lake air should be bracing this time of year."

Wrong again. An atmospheric inversion had settled on the area. The air felt tepid and soupy, unusually warm for November. No breeze. We walked hand in hand and looked at the glut of overpriced designer merchandise in the windows of the Michigan Avenue shops and got depressed about the '80s. It was difficult to see, as an enormous new high-rise cast shadows that put the street in perpetual twilight. The inversion meant that car and bus fumes settled near the ground.

But this was our anniversary! Party time!

We made reservations for a late dinner at Ciel Bleu. Because the rooftop restaurant overlooked the lake, the view outside the windows was mainly a black void. No matter; we were there for the food. While we were waiting, a Continental man kept putting rolls on our plates.

Fritz kept eating them, and I realized as I watched him that he was getting sleepy. "Don't eat too many of those, or you won't be hungry," I warned.

It didn't matter. Remember what I said about European people, at least those of the southern variety, being small? It's no wonder. They're stunted from malnutrition. Our dinners each featured about three tiny pieces of meat accompanied by six perfect little carrots. Fritz stared disconsolately at his meal as if expecting scalloped potatoes and gravy to erupt from some hidden lode of cholesterol.

And so it went. After dinner Fritz fell asleep on the bed, while I perused the hotel-chain magazine and read about how Spanish gastronomes just *love* dolphin embryos as part of their *tapas.* No wonder Sir Francis Drake defeated the Armada in 1588. While the Brits dined on sensible hardtack and limes, the Spaniards were writhing in pain from the last stages of salmonella poisoning.

I do not wish to imply that the trip was a bust, because no weekend alone with my husband is a bust. Also, I did buy my squeeze a handsome patterned sweater at Bloomingdale's, and he still looks mighty handsome in it. Wears it every Thanksgiving. We even laugh about it now, how I had to tell the maid with the "cordial turndown" to hand me the mints through the crack in the chained door and never mind turning down the sheets because HE was sleeping off all those rolls. I mean, who's in their hotel room at nine on a Friday night?

And I learned a couple things from our weekend with Armand . . . and Emilio . . . and Jean-Jacques-Luc and the rest. One, as if you had not already guessed, is that my husband is not what you might call a boulevardier, a bon vivant. In the early days of our marriage I plied him with expensive gifts from Brooks Brothers—pajamas (which ripped), sterling silver keychains (which got bent), rosewood hairbrushes (he prefers combs). I thought that's what you were "supposed" to do when you were in love. He has since said, "I don't care what I get, just that *you* give it to me!" I would suggest expensive restaurants, and he would go along, but I could tell he wasn't really enjoying himself. I thought that's where you were "supposed" to go when you were in the honeymoon phase of your relationship.

This is my husband: One of his favorite pastimes is checking out the ad supplements in the Sunday paper and saying things like, "Venture has a sale on rubber bath mats. Should we pick one up?" If I'm making a stir-fry with rice and vegetables and a *soupcon* of meat, he'll say, "How about adding a hot dog?" He buys clothes for himself at garage sales and likes white bread and hard physical work and messing around in the basement. He wishes we could go camping sometime, like his family did when he was a kid.

To tell you the truth, I am not much of a bonne vivante either, although I like to think I can do without hot dogs in stir-fry and my idea of roughing it is a hotel room without pay-per-view. Here's how I try to have it both ways: On our last anniversary, Fritz and I went out together and I bought him a fashionably garish necktie, because all his ties are old-fashioned rep style. The tie cost seven ninety-nine. At Wal-Mart. And afterward we picked up submarine sandwiches for dinner and took them home and ate them at our kitchen table.

That's my husband's idea of a really great getaway, bless 'im. Maybe it's not what's expected. Maybe it's not what you're supposed to do when you want to wax romantic. But when you talk romance . . . I guess I think we're not hurting in that department. Even if the kisses are sometimes smeared with mustard.

---

First appeared in *Marriage Partnership* Magazine, Summer 1989.

# *GOD OUR MAKER DOTH PROVIDE...*

THIS IS ALMOST UNBELIEVABLE. Here I am, slightly past forty, and this is only my second time roasting a Thanksgiving turkey. Let's see. Pull out the giblets and simmer for gravy. Rub butter all over the bird and inside the cavity. Ponder why a pink, uncooked turkey looks so disconcertingly lifelike. I almost want to apologize to it.

Here's the stuffing. Thank you, Mr. Pepperidge! Add celery, water chestnuts, raisins, herbs. Yet more butter. I like the tactility of this, shoving the gloppy concoction into the bird with my bare hands. No other way to do it.

There. I cover the bird with a loose tent of foil and pop it in the oven. I remember my mother having to get up at the crack of dawn to start the turkey. It took *hours* to cook. Of course, we went out to a turkey farm back then. Maybe the fowl were tougher. I used to hate the sound of the birds gobbling back in the sheds. They sounded like a bunch of feathered car alarms going off.

For years, long after I was married, Thanksgiving meant going home to Mom and Dad's – helping Mom bake the pies the night before, waking Dad from his evening nap so he could come downstairs and do the taste test on the pumpkin filling, waking to the mingled smell of silver polish and roasting Tom. Dad always polished every piece in the house, whether we were going to use it or not. Usually a card table was set up to accommodate overflow.

And overflow we did, after eating. The menu, by Dad's decree, rarely changed. It was understood that this was his favorite holiday, so we cooked to please him – rich, creamy foods like corn casserole, creamed onions, candied sweet potatoes.

My table will be a little healthier – broccoli instead of corn casserole, cranberry-oatmeal muffins instead of white rolls. But much will be the same. The homemade pies sit in the fridge. I polished the silver and cleaned house from top to bottom. Amanda will eat only the turkey and mashed potatoes. Someone will comment on how it's a good thing we don't eat this way all the time. Someone else will remark that they hope the roads are OK for getting home.

Now I can relax a moment. Fritz has taken Amanda to the market to pick up a few last-minute items and leave the sweaty hostess in peace. I sit at the kitchen table with my coffee. Fritz and I have already observed one of our traditional Turkey Day customs, sharing with each other – and with God – what we are especially thankful for this year. Gratitude, we agree, sometimes needs to be affirmed out loud and in specifics. Some of the things we're grateful for are the same year in and year out: no major health problems, a warm, comfortable house when so many are homeless, our marriage and God's gift of our daughter. Others are more specific: the end of the Cold War, job opportunities, new friends that have come into our lives during the past year, Amanda's teacher. This is no time to present God with a long list of petitions, we believe. It's a day to recognize exactly what He has done for us—whether or not we deserve it.

We're so blessed it's almost embarrassing, I reflect now. Why have we been favored with such abundance when so many worldwide have so little? Why were we born in America and not Somalia? Why have we been spared the agony of alcoholism, chronic illness, drastic financial reversal? Money is always tight, but somehow we scrape by, and that's enough for us. Why did we grow up with healthy models of marriage when so many now come out of broken homes? Why does our own marriage work most of the time?

"Why me?" can apply to joy as well as pain. It's a mystery. And it feels like a challenge: Much will be expected from those to whom much has been given. Husband these gifts wisely. Make the talents grow into something.

Speaking of husbands, we celebrated our anniversary the other day, quietly—some years we just cannot do a big splash, and this is one of those years, not with me doing Thanksgiving and an upcoming birthday party for Amanda. But how nice of him to run to the store for me. He does things like this all the time, little kindnesses that add up into something very big. He's easy to live with. He's been known to be romantic. He lets me lean on him – more than he leans on me, and sometimes I worry about that. He does the laundry and I clean. Best of all, I think as I drink my coffee and check off the to-do list, it feels like we're still growing together after all these years. I once read that if you can make it to fifteen years you're – not home free, maybe, but much is resolved. It feels like we're getting there.

I look out the window over the kitchen sink. It's a gray, raw day; they're predicting a chance of snow for later. I hope it holds off until everyone is safely home. Then I hope it snows like crazy. We're due for a really authentic winter. Amanda's never seen a true blizzard.

The oven timer ticks; the refrigerator cycles on. All this is so sweet, so familiar – the view of our neighbor's tall trees through the window, the sound of a passing car, the faint scent of Mop-and-Glo rising from the scrubbed kitchen floor. And I know Fritz feels the same way. One of his greatest gifts is his ability to be content with the simple, the everyday. He has taught me a great deal about this, and in so doing has helped to calm a spirit inclined to be restless and dissatisfied. At the same time, I've helped him to strive, to push. It's a nice tension.

I hear the slamming of car doors. Did he pick up the whipping cream? The paper towels? The nutmeg?

He did. He also got Amanda a candy bar; I see the evidence on her face. Oh, well. It's a long time until we eat, and today is not the day to worry about nutritional correctness. I give him a big hug. "What's that for?" he asks, surprised. (I know him; he expected me to be agitated and panicky, as is my usual custom before hosting a gathering.)

"Oh, just because," I say. Then I do the same for Amanda, who is not surprised. That is as it should be. So, this Thanksgiving morning, is everything else.

# *WINTER*

# *MY HUSBAND, THE METABOLIC MIRACLE*

"IS THERE MORE?"

I looked at my husband through morning-bleared eyes, or maybe I hadn't put in my contacts yet. "What do you mean, 'more'?" I felt like the mean guy in *Oliver*! when Oliver Twist pathetically asks for more gruel in his English-boy accent: "Please, sir . . . can I have some more?"

"You just had a bowl of Kix and fruit. Isn't that enough?"

"No. I'm still hungry."

"Well, *I'm* full."

"You're on a diet. You have a little stomach. I need to gain weight. Could you make me an egg or something?"

I sighed. Who am I to let my mate go to work in

the cold with that lean and hungry look? "Here. Have some yogurt. People shouldn't eat too many eggs."

I've heard couples say that together they've lost and gained hundreds of pounds. I know husbands and wives who go on Slim-Fast together, have Doritos-and-salsa binges together, jog together, do Nautilus together. Fritz's and my diet history is somewhat different, however. He, you see, has the metabolism of a whippet. He eats ice cream every night. Three pork chops are standard fare, with maybe some leftover spaghetti on the side. He also insists on three sitdown meals a day when we're all home. And he's as trim and hard as an Olympic sprinter. He probably weighs less than he did in high school. My mother thinks we should try to patent the secret of Fritz's metabolism and market it to one of the pharmaceutical companies.

My metabolism isn't exactly sluggish, but if I consumed even a fraction of what he eats I would balloon to Delta Burke-like proportions. Better check in at the weigh station, lady. So I exercise a lot and have found that eating half a can of white tuna fish and a banana, on the run, is better for me than sitting down to a full repast, because that feels like fun and when eating is fun one tends to do too much of it.

This would not be a problem if I were single. If I were single I would live on bottled water and oatmeal and dine with MacNeil and Lehrer as my companions. But, as I am not single, I set the table, light candles, and serve meals, off plates, from the four basic food groups, all the while trying to satisfy the nutritional agendas of three different people: Fritz, who needs and wants to eat more; Amanda, who needs to eat right; and the wife and mother, who needs to eat less. We eat sitting down, enjoying companionable conversation. It's fun. Sometimes too much so.

We learned this when we were first married. Back then we did what every couple does: we porked out. I collected cookbooks and was forever coming up with new taste treats for Mr. Right. Stews, casseroles, biscuits, fried potatoes with sugar . . . and the results were predictable. We have home movies of ourselves, since transferred to video, that no one will ever see. Here are Mr. and Mrs. Hippo visiting Niagara Falls. See Babar and his queen lumbering along on their walk. Observe the happy round faces.

Gradually the cookbooks went back onto the bookshelf and the weight came off—his faster than mine, in keeping with the cruel reality that it is easier for men to get thin than it is for women, because women are supposed to carry around extra fat for nourishing babies or something. I walk everywhere, strenuously. Amanda will sometimes ask, "Why are we walking to school, Mommy? It's snowing. Everyone else is driving." "Put your hood up," I puff. I try to eat to live, not the other way around. And I still have thighs. Fritz drinks whole milk, enjoys lying down and accepts third helpings. He could lose weight in his sleep. If he had his body fat tested the count would be in the negative numbers. My husband, the medical marvel.

I know his mother thinks I don't feed her boy properly. She won't say it, but her actions betray her. When we visit her she plies him with roast beef, potatoes, and gravy for dinner and cooks him stevedore breakfasts. (Which I, with the enthusiasm generated by someone else's cooking, also partake of. Another muffin? Sure.)

It doesn't help that many of our social activities have revolved around the church. I don't know if it's because traditionally many forms of entertainment were frowned upon for Christians, so eating became an acceptable alternative, but God's people tend to take the "taste and see" command quite literally. When my husband was a student pastor we were in a church where many members were older, German, with small-town roots. And they were *great* cooks, and they loved to invite the young minister and his wife to eat. (They knew a receptive audience when they saw it.) Fritz and I still talk about the time the Bohner sisters had us over one Saturday morning and served those refrigerator crescent rolls steeped in brown-sugar glaze. They've become part of our oral tradition. As has the Cool Whip/pineapple/instant pudding/graham cracker dessert that crowned the annual church board dinner. And the Chicken Divan someone always brought to potlucks.

It's a good thing we left *that* church. I tremble to think of the implications, had we remained.

Periodically the church we're in now holds hot-dog lunches on Sundays. The idea is for members and friends to enjoy a light meal following worship and Sunday School. The last time we went, I got to talking to different people and—intentionally—did not have much time to eat. While I was so engaged, I noticed my husband returning to the hot dog table. Once. Twice. Thrice. As we were driving home I asked him, curiously, "How many hot dogs did you eat?" "Oh, eight," he said.

"Did anyone SAY anything?"

"Oh, I doubt if anyone noticed."

People are starving in Mozambique, and my husband is gobbling hot dogs that could go to the needy. But this is how he thinks about food: If it's composed of identifiable animal, vegetable, or grain matter, and it's not moving, it's fair game. Whereas I, like many women, am so diet-habituated I have this killjoy attitude, that eating is a necessary, somewhat embarrassing practice best performed in private, something like cleaning one's ears with a Q-tip. Secretly, of course, I really like to cook and eat. I even eat airline food. Even the roll. Which is why most of the time I steel myself like a Marine in training, to take the rugged road of self-denial.

Not only that, but there are budgetary considerations involved here. I would like, occasionally, to have enough chicken for another meal. He thinks it's lying there clucking "Eat me! Now!" I suspect he just doesn't want to be faced with leftovers for supper.

So here we are unquestionably confronting colliding dietary imperatives. As the wife, I am supposed to treat hubby right with plentiful home-cooked meals. And I want to make him happy. I really do. But *thirds?*

I guess we're still blundering our way toward compromise. He eats a moderate amount at mealtime and enjoys a hefty snack later. I fill up on green beans or salad and let him do the dishes so I don't dive into the leftover rice or potatoes while cleaning up. There are no easy answers, as someone once said. Especially in winter, when you feel like you owe it to yourself to stoke up on calories so you don't get hypothermia or something.

And, in a world where nutritional wet blankets abound, Fritz's unbridled, joyful abandon while eating is kind of fun. O taste and see . . . but not *too* often.

# THE HARD EMBRACE OF THE BABE

IS THERE ANYTHING quite like a clear winter night?

We are looking up at the stars, my husband and I. The constellations are clearly visible – striding Orion, with Taurus the bull behind and Sirius at their heels. The Pleiades, all seven sisters. Rocking Cassiopeia. The Big Dipper. And more. The effect is somewhat dizzying, even fearsome, as if the stars are bending toward us to check us out. The human mind cannot take too much vastness. I understand why it is dangerous to behold the blazing face of God.

We have come here to the woods for a walk. Christmas approaches, and we agreed that this year we would spend at least a little time seeking

Christmas in the silent cold of field and forest. The silence here is deep; the air so clear, so crisp it almost twangs. Pluck a star and hear a high note; pick a bare branch and play a deeper note. The loudest sound is the crunching of the frozen grass under our booted feet.

Tonight, the darkness owns the world. We have come to the time of the winter solstice, when the sun is in retreat. As we were driving here I noticed the sunset, the sun a halfhearted lemony ball way to the south, giving up as the purple dark approached from the east. I remarked to Fritz that there was something odd and subarctic about the effect. Electricity, car lights, and central heating have diminished the power of the darkness in our minds, taken away the terror that the ancients must have felt. Here, though, the night is almost a presence. It will not be denied.

Here too we try to come close to how it felt on the night Jesus was born. The stars in the Judean desert . . . just imagine! The shepherds knew each of them – except the one that dwarfed all the others. Brighter than Sirius. Outshining Venus. What must they have thought? To top it off, a dazzling being appeared in the sky. No wonder they were "sore afraid"! It isn't every day that the Lord Himself descends. Look upon His face: no more a terrible blaze, but the soft features of an Infant.

Christmas in our time has become so cozy, so comfortable, that it is easy to forget the danger and discomfort that accompanied the birth in Bethlehem. Mary, a teenager great with Child, bouncing along on a donkey. The magi on their snorting camels, heavily cloaked against the desert chill. The rage of mad Herod. The stink of the stable. Maybe the wall of the cave dripped water. Surely Mary's labor was painful.

But we've domesticated Christmas, turned the wildness into a comfy celebration of family, and taken away the peril and wonder so that the only danger seems to be the trip of a mythical jolly old elf from the North Pole, complete with radio reports from air-traffic controllers of "sightings" of an airborne sleigh. And certainly, the Newenhuyses fall in step with all the family warmth and silly customs and birthday-party-for-Jesus sentiment. But we've also discussed how our world—and, too often, the church—has elevated the

Kodak-moment mentality above the earthquake of the Incarnation. Instead of greeting cards that read "From our house to your house," maybe the expression should be "From My heaven to My earth."

Like the stars, it's almost too much for mere man to comprehend cognitively. I think this is why we have come to tramp the fields: not so much to commune with nature—it's too cold for that—but, somehow, to move a little nearer to the Creator Himself. Someone once told me that the reason millions throng the national parks every year, hike the backcountry, even picnic by a lakeside is that we're instinctively stumbling toward the throne, though too many of us are blind to the real glory behind the purple mountain majesties.

For this reason, of course, the Babe was sent, to sweep the mud from our vision, to take our pain and wrongness onto His shoulders. As we step along the path, we speak of this, albeit in short bursts because it's too cold to talk a lot. It's taking all we have to walk and stay warm. That's all right; the companionship is enough.

It's difficult to fight the Christmas machine.

There are times I feel that "they" (the world) have stolen the holiday from "us" (the Christ-ones) . . . profaned it, robbed it of its real meaning to the point where we, the church visible, cave in to the Hallmark-Bing Crosby-Toys "R" Us holiday juggernaut. Then I get really depressed and hope such usurpation never happens to "our" Easter. Bah, humbug!

And yet . . . are those who revel in "the spirit of Christmas" really reaching for an infinitely more powerful Spirit, something like the millions gaping at the Grand Canyon? And further, do we as believers completely understand what it means to follow the Baby?

I'm glad it's so cold tonight. It's a needful reminder of who is in charge. It strikes me that the taming of Christmas has obscured the awesome reality of the challenge of following Christ, the way winter windows fog up and obscure the lamplight inside. Sure, there's the joy, the peace, the laughter. But there's also sacrifice, inconvenience, the need to make hard choices. Maybe that's why the suffering church in Africa is growing.

They too will be celebrating in a few days—

without snow, but also without John Denver specials (I hope). The embrace of the Babe stretches around His world.

And around the two of us. Just like last spring, when I played Mary and Fritz created the role of Quintilius the centurion, I think how glad I am that I am not on this journey alone. Another human being, heart of my heart, is helping me along—literally—steadying me when I slide on an icy patch, sharing the wonder.

Now my toes are starting to grow numb and the cold has penetrated my mittens. It is time to head back. Tomorrow, alas, we will have to shop and bake and join the scurrying Christmas crowds. But now we hold hands, say a quick prayer of thanksgiving and, under the watch of Orion, return to our car, content that, for a little while at least, we have made life a little harder for ourselves—the way it was on the night that split time forever.

# *WHEN TRADITIONS COLLIDE*

THREE LITTLE PAJAMA-CLAD CHILDREN sit at the top of the stairs. From below a voice booms, "Uh-oh! I see a lot of good things!"

Their mother hands them all a glass of orange juice. They are restless, fidgety. "Can we come?"

"Not yet."

Lights! Action! "NOW!"

They burst downstairs, elbowing each other out of the way. And there it is, the lit Christmas tree! And look what's under it: big boxes and small! Dolls and books and Lincoln Log sets and air hockey games and some things too big to wrap.

They dive in, searching for packages tagged for them, pawing other boxes out of the way like a dog digging a hole. "I got Chatty Cathy!" "Look, *Little*

*House in the Big Woods!*" Clothes from relatives are tossed aside. They never fit anyway. "Saucer sleds!" A real microscope! Stockings filled with watches and pens and charm bracelets!

All the while, their parents, who I now know were exhausted from staying up until 2 A.M. making all this possible, sit and drink coffee. They'll open their few gifts, including our presents to them – a tie clip for Dad, who never wears tie clips; Woolworth's perfume for Mom, who prefers Arpege – later.

My Christmas, circa 1960.

Another family a few miles away has already opened their gifts. They did it the night before, on Christmas Eve as the Scandinavians do. "Santa" came knocking at the door and walked in, to hand packages to the eagerly waiting children. Here's one for Fritz! Everyone waits and watches while he opens it. Then everyone waits further as it gets passed around so everyone can ooh and aah. A Landmark book! Who's it from? Here's one for Grandma. Let's see the card. Oh, a scarf! "Let's be sure to save the paper," says Mom, carefully folding it for reuse.

Package after package, slowly doled out, opened with proper decorum, handed around the circle as if the family were women at a baby shower.

My husband's Christmas, about the same year.

Two families, living not far from each other, in many ways very similar—but with radically divergent holiday traditions.

Fifteen years later, the eldest son and eldest daughter of each family would meet and eventually marry. One month after the wedding, they—we—would experience the full force of the drama: When *traditions collide.*

We woke early on Christmas morning, woozy after just a few hours' sleep. My new husband was student pastor at a large church and we had been up late with midnight services the night before. But our presence—and our presents—were expected at both his and my parents' homes that day, so we hauled out with our station wagon loaded and made the hour's drive eastward.

At my parents' house everything was right and familiar. Hugs and coffee and the Christmas cards displayed in the entryway just as they always had been. As usual Dad had picked out one of the biggest, fullest trees on the lot. I showed Fritz "my" childhood ornaments, the stocking my grandmother had embroidered for me when I was a baby.

And we took the plunge, diving into the pile of gifts, seeing which boxes had our names on them. Oh, we took the time to hand some packages to others. But it was pretty much the same joyous chaos as it always had been, every man for himself, no one playing Santa, making you wait. And no one saving wrapping paper.

Then we went to my mother-in-law's. Christmas cards were not displayed, but there was a box of Christmas tissue in the powder room. The tree was small and decorated with lights that had bubbles in them. The wreath on the door was not fragrant balsam, but artificial. I noted all this with something approaching dismay. This was *different.* This was not the usual, ordained way of things.

And we had to eat before we opened gifts. At *my* house first things came first.

By the time dinner was over, I was feeling thoroughly churlish and out of sync, not to mention exhausted. My husband, on the other hand, was enjoying himself immensely. We proceeded to the living room.

"Sit down," my mother-in-law said. "Fritz, will you be Santa?"

I didn't want him to be Santa. I wanted him to sit next to me. But he accepted his assignment with alacrity. "Here's a present to Mother from Grandma!" We all sat and watched as she opened whatever it was. The gift was passed around, duly commented on. "Let's see the card!" someone said. The card was passed around.

And around and around we went. One after another. "Be careful opening the paper," my mother-in-law gently reproved me as I started the Cody rip. *Save the paper?* I thought. "And save that box," she added.

The Ritual of Opening—stately, measured—took about two hours. I had never experienced anything like it. Worse, my husband seemed to be enjoying it. This was his way, after all. I felt almost betrayed. Where was *our* Christmas? Is this what was in store for us every holiday? The attention to presents, especially since we were all adults, seemed materialistic, almost inappropriate.

We were spending the night there. As we got ready for bed, Fritz asked, "So what did you think about your first Newenhuyse Christmas?"

"Do you ALWAYS do it like this?" I burst out. "Why does everybody have to just sit there?"

"I knew you weren't having a good time," he said. "I hope no one else noticed."

I was not going to find much sympathy from his quarter, I could tell. I turned out the light and wished we were like couples whose extended families live a thousand miles away.

Since that first year we have done Christmas with increasing success, although the road to true celebration of the Savior's birth has been bumpy. There was, for example, the year of the "K Mart Christmas." We had moved into a new pastorate early in December and had no time to shop, so my gifts from my husband consisted of a set of baking dishes, steel shelving and a padded toilet seat because the one in my bathroom was cracked. I cried. He was bewildered, because he truly thought he was doing me a service. (The next year I got a fluffy robe. I still wear it.)

There was the year we decided to send Christmas cards to practically everyone we knew, including many people in the church we were serving. It wound up taking hours and hours and costing about $75.

There was the year our daughter was born, only three weeks before Christmas. The weather had turned bitterly cold and, therefore, people had to come to *us*.

And throughout, we were slowly coming to terms with each other's family traditions—and developing a few of our own. Turning out all the lights except those on the tree, lighting candles and reading Luke's Nativity account on Christmas Eve. Participating in the children's service at church. Laughing about our yearly argument. (Me: "There aren't enough lights on the tree. Look, there's a bare spot." He: "I'm not going to go out and buy more.")

Some of the faces around the Christmas table have changed. My dad and Fritz's grandma, both of whom loved the day so much, are no longer with us, but an assortment of children is. I've learned that it's kind of nice to take gift-opening slowly, and my mother-in-law jokes about the same recycled boxes showing up year after year. The Christmas Kleenex box has disappeared, and I kind of miss it. ("Oh, that was so old, I think I finally threw it away!" said Fritz's mother.)

And, this year, I'm considering hosting Christmas dinner—something we've never done. It's time, you see, to say "thank you" to all those other dear people who have fed and served and feted us over the years. Thank God they're only a few miles away. Maybe I can get my mother-in-law's recipe for creamed spinach.

# *FLOWERS IN THE SNOW*

SHE WAS VAGUELY FAMILIAR. Small, with tired, doe-soft brown eyes and a gentle manner. In her seventies. Then, when she started talking about her husband, I snapped to recognition. Our neighbor, whose spouse had been an invalid for years. "He's . . . not doing very well," she said without any prompting from me. "He doesn't have any veins in his legs. They're trying a new procedure."

She struggled for composure. "He just sits. He likes to read. It's so hard. . . ."

We were at a neighborhood block party, standing in the street. The evening was mild, but I was thinking of winter as she continued. Clearly she needed to talk. She told me how twenty years ago she had found him sitting in a chair, just staring.

He was only fifty-eight or so at the time. According to the neurologist, he had a slow-growing brain tumor. Several operations followed. Other things, apparently, had gone wrong.

"My daughter says I should get someone to come in during the night," she said in her quiet voice. "He wakes up and I don't get any sleep."

I looked around at the party, at the young couples laughing, talking about their work, their children. The kids rode up and down the blocked-off street, such fun to be able to career around without threat of traffic. Youth. Health. The future.

But you never know.

"I don't want to put him in a nursing home," she went on. "He needs to be here."

I nodded. There was a pause, during which I cast about for something to say. What do you mean, the Lord has been good to you? . . . I'm sure glad my dad didn't live to be an invalid . . . I wish I could make it all better for you.

I looked at their well-kept yard and said politely, "Your yard always looks so nice."

"Oh, my sister does that. You know she lives with us."

The sister, if anything even more gentle, joined us. Seeing the two of them together I was reminded of characters in a book, sitting fanning themselves on their front porch and handing out lemonade to visiting children. They were so soft, so small, they drifted around like pieces of milkweed fluff, the traveling seeds I called "fairies" when I was little. I felt little now, a child about to discover something.

"We have a garden in back," said the sister.

"Oh."

"It's a cottage garden. Maybe you'd like to see it sometime." Her tone implied that I was probably too busy.

An impulse seized me: "Could we see it now? I love gardens!"

"Why, certainly."

I was unprepared for what I saw. Behind the prim white house, bordered just so by its hostas and evergreens, burst a riot of color, scent, *delight.* Zinnias, marigolds, climbing nasturtiums, lilies, sweet-smelling lavender, many more I did not recognize. It was like opening the diary of a spinster home economics teacher and finding poetry of tumbled, eloquent passion. I wondered if Emily Dickinson kept a garden like this, behind her father's house in Amherst. Or maybe Emily just *dreamed* of a garden like this.

The garden was abundant and informal, in the English style. Crimsons and peaches and indigos and cornflowers and violets and magentas, all the Crayola palette. I had rarely seen such profusion outside a professionally landscaped estate. The garden was not large, just a wedge at the corner of the house . . . but it was intense, intimate.

"It's from a packet of seeds called Monet's Palette," said the sister. "I didn't know what anything was going to be."

A mystery garden! Now it wasn't just Emily Dickinson, it was sickly, orphaned Mary Lennox, discovering the key to the Secret Garden. I crumbled some lavender leaves between my fingers and wished I could make sachet.

Then I noticed the tomato plants. "You have tomatoes!" I exclaimed.

"Would you like some?" asked the man's wife.

I would. Fritz had accidentally mowed over our one surviving plant, for which the prognosis had been dubious at best. She disappeared into the house. I noticed the television was on, and wondered if the invalid husband ever came out to sit by the garden. I hoped so.

We talked a little longer; I was drawn to these sisters, sensing a fineness of spirit in both. But dusk was settling over us and I needed to round up my child and go home. I told them I would be back to draw inspiration from the garden. "Any time," they said.

The party was breaking up. I looked around for Amanda and thought about the encounter. I wasn't sure where to file it; I had started out pitying the wife, chained to her house and her sick mate, hardly getting out for days at a time. Now I wondered whether this was the unforgiving January terminus of a long marriage, or a gracious April. The sisters, and their flowers, had confounded my neat categories.

Hope. Maybe that was it.

Not logical hope, as in, I hope Amanda can go to a good Christian college, or I hope the rain will stop. If she works hard enough and financing can be arranged, Amanda may well get into a Wheaton or a Gordon. The rain always does stop.

No – this was something far more powerful. This was the hope that plants a garden even as the doctor is shaking her head and saying, "There's nothing more we can do." This is the hope that shimmers with eternity's promise. It's more than the so-called unquenchable human spirit; I've seen too many human spirits be thoroughly quenched. Such hope comes only from God, and cannot be explained. It's a bouquet growing in a blizzard. And I call it remarkable.

I walked into the house. "Look, Fritz!" I called. "Come see the beautiful tomatoes."

# THEY SHALL MOUNT UP ON ROBIN'S WINGS

HAVE YOU EVER FELT like you were witnessing a private moment that was so special, so intimate that it bordered on the holy and you had to turn away, because you had no business blundering onto this sacred ground?

I was sitting in my dad's room in a convalescent center. We thought he was convalescing, but he would die there within the week. He had had brain surgery. The surgery had "worked," in that he had not died on the table and the cyst causing some balance and memory problems had been removed. But a seventy-year-old man is at risk for all kinds of things following a major operation, and they don't get more major than someone opening up your skull. Dad battled back from pneumonia, soaring fevers, systemic septicemia. He did not battle back from the strokes, possibly multiple, he suffered as a result of the surgery.

There was really nothing more the hospital could do. He was too weak to enter a rehab program. So there he lay, in the last place he had ever wanted to go, an alien environment of strangers and old people (Dad? Old? Never!) and weary nurses who saw too few children and too little hope.

And there was my mother, visiting him every day. Talking to him. Kissing him. Trying to get him interested in watching the color TV she had bought for him. Tossing a rubber ball to him, which the therapist had said would be exercise of a sort.

It was not supposed to finish like this after forty-four years of marriage. They had been talking about selling the big house and retiring to Cape Cod, where all the grown kids and grandkids could come visit. Dad would paint and Mom could read, walk the beach, make friends. They'd both live to be eighty-five or ninety and go peacefully in their sleep, within a few months of each other.

Oh, they needed each other so badly. And we needed both of them. We weren't ready to be orphaned.

But now I sat in a chair on one side of Dad's bed, happy just to be there for him, while my mother sat on the other side, the side he seemed to have more strength in. She was talking to him about some problem she had run into at her job. (He had been wanting her to quit.) His eyes, those fierce greenish hawk eyes, were fixed on her. I wasn't sure how much he was absorbing. Her face was drawn and pale after months of what's-wrong-with-Dad, Dad's-sick, Dad-has-to-go-to-the-hospital, Dad-can't-come-home.

Then, wordlessly, he reached out his one good hand to hers, drew her hand toward his lips and kissed it. This man, so ill, was comforting the wife of his youth.

I couldn't watch any longer. I was intruding on a holy place meant only for two. Don't mind me, I'm just your daughter. I'll be going now. I slipped quietly into the bathroom.

I shall never forget the picture of those two, loving each other in that awful, sterile room with the respirator clicking and wheezing and the late-winter sky darkening with the onset of night. I'm glad too that the picture lives only in my mind and on my heart, and not on video or in a snapshot. Some memories are too precious to hand over to Kodak.

I was to replay that non-Kodak moment many times in the weeks to come. I was to replay many moments (and look at many photos) in the ensuing weeks. For, a few days after this, we were awakened at about 6 on a Saturday morning by a phone call.

Many of us, I think, run through our minds how it will be when we hear a parent has left us. The sudden phone call from a sibling, or the vigil at the hospital with a chaplain or doctor in scrubs breaking the news. You run it through your mind, but you're never prepared.

Fritz answered the phone, as he always does when calls come at odd and threatening times. "Hi, Bev," he said sleepily. "How's Dick?"

I sat bolt upright in bed. *Danger-danger-danger* was thudding through me.

Pause. "Oh, no . . . I'll let you talk to Betsey."

He brought me the cordless phone. I looked the question at him. He nodded.

The warrior had fallen. Dad had passed away just minutes ago, as dawn was peeking over the east on this day that was not quite winter, not quite spring. The nurse had called Mom, who was leaving for the convalescent center momentarily. "How are you?" I asked idiotically. How would *I* feel if I was facing life without my spouse of nearly five decades?

"I'm holding up," she said, not sounding as if she was holding up. "Could you call Todd and Annie?" My brother and sister out East. My other sister, Barbara, was somewhere cruising the Spanish Main with her husband; Mom was trying to get hold of them.

"Sure. Then we'll get someone to stay with Amanda and we'll be right up."

Things to do. Things to do. I prayed for sustenance (you never think you're going to be the one breaking the news, and there is no easy way to do it) and made the calls. Shower. Dress. Make the bed. No breakfast. No time.

When we got to Dad's room the door was

closed. Mom was already there. With Dad. We embraced. Dad was still . . . warm. But oh, so still. I broke into sobs over him and wished we were someplace other than this building of strangers. I wished we were home and Dad was in his bed, next to his radio and reading glasses, and we could all keen together like old Irish biddies, or sit *shiva* like Jewish women. Draw the drapes, hang the crepe, wear the weeds of grief. Observe the proper and prolonged rituals.

But people don't die in their beds as much as they used to. Death comes when a machine stops beeping and the line goes flat and a nurse reading a magazine at her station glances up and notices that the machine doesn't seem to be working. We don't always go surrounded by our kin, and you can't wail in a nursing home. And if you do, be quick about it. Go home! Life is for the living. He would want it that way.

Not Dad. He'd want people to shout and scream. He was never real stoic; the Irish don't do understatement.

My mother asked if I'd like to be alone with him. I would. And I am eternally grateful to God that I was able to say farewell, say some prayers, help send my father on his way home.

Later, needing fresh air, we walked around the grounds of the center. It was cold, but the early-March sun was bright. "Listen!" I said, stopping. "I hear a robin."

We went in search of it, and found a big male, perched in a berry tree right next to the front door of the place, caroling his heart out. He flew from one tree to the next, never going far, always singing. It was the first robin any of us had seen that year.

Celtic tradition has it that when a warrior falls in battle, bagpipers play at his funeral, piping him to the next world. We listened to the robin a long time. "I'm SURE he's piping Dad home," I said, weeping. And my mother smiled.

Winter into spring. Death to life. If someone had written the script I should have thought the symbolism heavyhanded, obvious. But this robin was real, and the season was on the turn. What a wonderful finish!

I have thought often since then about "finishing well," closing out your life as a couple with love and dignity and devotion. Mom and Dad finished well. Despite a marriage that was sometimes stormy (remember what I said about Dad's lack of understatement?), they stayed the course. I remember my father hugging my mother and saying, "I'm like the eagle. I mate for life." (It was this declaration that prompted me to suggest the Isaiah 40 passage, "They shall mount up with wings as eagles," as one of the texts for Dad's memorial service.)

My parents could look back and say, *And it was good. It was hard, but it was good.* Not everyone can make that statement.

I hope I can. I hope that someday, if my husband or I get sick and find ourselves in an institutional room with a respirator breathing for us and an IV tube feeding us . . . I hope that we too can reach out and take the other's hand. Sometimes, that says enough.

# *SPRING AGAIN*

# *AND IN THE BEGINNING...AGAIN*

AND SO WE COME AROUND AGAIN to another spring.

It's been a rough winter. I'm glad for spring. Glad for thunderstorms. Glad our taxes are done. Glad baseball is back; somehow, when the season starts it seems like all's right with the world. Maybe this will be the year our two teams make it. I'd be happy with even *one* making it. Hope springs eternal.

And spring is hope eternal.

My husband just had a birthday. We've gotten into the habit of using certain "as old as" yardsticks—older than the Beatles were when they broke up, as old as our parents were when they sent kids to college, older than teachers we thought were ancient. John F. Kennedy is another benchmark. On my last birthday I said, "You know, I'm now as old as Kennedy was when he was elected." My husband rejoined, "On my next birthday, I'll be as old as Kennedy was when he was shot." Not everyone would understand that kind of humor. I laughed uproariously.

The older you get, the more aware you are of the passage of time; therefore, the more grateful you are for spring. Fall used to be my favorite season, but lately I've leaned toward spring. Fall announces that the end is near. Those blazing trees don't fool me one bit. I welcome the return of warmth. I don't even mind—much—teenage boys driving around with their cassette decks tuned to eardrum-hemorrhage levels. Seems sort of friendly.

I hold on to the renewal that spring pledges; it feels like you've once again made it through an ordeal, that God is giving you another chance. I like it that spring comes regardless of anything we've done. It feels like God shedding His grace.

Another spring. The beginning of something.

What?

I don't know, and that's why I rejoice in the season. Anything can happen. The White Sox could go all the way. We might actually get around to digging up the worthless roses and planting something *productive,* like a vegetable garden. The check could be in the mail when they say it will be. Maybe we'll make a new friend. The very sense of possibilities is rejuvenating.

On the other hand, the light at the end of the tunnel could be an oncoming train. We won't think about that now, though. Today, let's not be older and sobered up by life's lessons.

Fritz is always going on about getting older. He knows it makes me laugh. He stares in the mirror and says, "Look at me! I'm getting grey hair. I have this gaunt face and these lines around my mouth. I look like I'm about sixty. Sometimes when I play basketball I fantasize that I collapse on the court and have to be carried off. I know guys my age who are grandfathers."

"But you still get zits," I tease. "There's life in the old guy yet."

I'll say!

Funny . . . we always come back to laughter.

*"See! The winter is past; the rains are over and gone. Flowers appear on the earth; the season of singing has come"* (Song 2:11-12).

The season of singing.

I started our story by sharing that first spring with its hopeless-romantic expectations. Well, we still have those expectations; only now, tempered by time, I'd call us hope*ful* romantics, not silly or unrealistic, but reaching for something deeper. Something that goes beyond surface symbols of romance— rings and candlelight and date nights. Fritz gave me an opal ring on my last birthday. I love opals, their pale fire and mysterious inner rainbows. It's my birthstone. But opals are soft and easily dislodged from their setting. When I jammed my hand into our old-fashioned wall mail slot to get the mail, the opal came off. I retrieved it and we got it reset, but the point is, rings get lost, fall apart, have to be cleaned. Candles burn down and get wax all over the table. Date nights cost money; besides, we're both morning people who fold after about 9. We're just as happy getting out into the yard in jeans and sweaters, Fritz sawing off dead limbs while I rake. It isn't exciting, but it's us. I have a pair of earrings he got me at K Mart. Cost a dollar on sale. They look great, and I cherish them as if they were emeralds.

In some ways we violate the advice in the Christian marriage books. We don't always have couple devotions. We can be haphazard about money. We have been known to put each other last, or at least behind child and careers and chores. I couldn't say if our marriage was "traditional" or "egalitarian"—probably both and neither and it depends. But something works for us, as it works for many other couples who find that successful marriage requires more than following a set of neat precepts.

Maybe *reality* works for us—a certain tough-minded acceptance that hard times will come, but if you hang on to God and to each other, you can weather the storms. And how better to appreciate gentle spring than to survive howling winter?

In fact, the most beautiful spring I can recall came after the worst winter in our area's history. We had had nearly a hundred inches of snow, all told. There was so much it didn't go away until April. When it melted, it revealed glowing green everywhere, green so vivid it was almost blue. The snow had done that, acted as fertilizer and protective insulator, and the world was a garden. As Oswald Chambers said, we do live by God's surprises!

That spring was our first as husband and wife. This is our fourteenth. We're still watching for those surprises—in the seasons and in each other. And, God willing, we'll be watching for many seasons to come. Come away, my love!